Women Behaving Courageously

WOMEN BEHAVING COURAGEOUSLY

How Gutsy Women, Young and Old, Are Transforming the World

Ann Andrews

Published by Activity Press

Contact author: www.annandrews.co.nz

A catalogue record for this book is available from the National Library of New Zealand.

CONTENTS

'What a wonderful read! Not only is this book superbly written; not only is it so very well researched; it's also a wonderful book because it is beautifully inspirational, without any maudlin hero-worship. Ann Andrews has taken us on a journey of introduction and encouragement, showing us that every woman behaves courageously when we live our truth, commit to our growth and fearlessly allow our stories to be shared with the world. Thank you Ann for this opportunity to explore our own courage, inspired, encouraged and guided by the choices so many women have made and are still making.'

Catherine Palin-Brinkworth
M.AppSci (Social Ecology), CSP, FIML
Leadership Speaker, Author, Mentor
Author of *The SHIFT Worker*

'Ann has tackled a huge topic and succeeded in presenting it with lightness and insight. She's a natural writer and a deep thinker who makes her points with great kindness and the occasional telling observation! She shares her 'warrior styles' for women so you can try each one on and see which one fits! And of course, she doesn't let you get away without actually taking some warrior actions! Despite her sometimes 'take-no-prisoners' material, woven throughout is a strong thread of kindness and practicality. This is a wonderful book!'

Clare Feeney
Author of *How to Change the World: A practical guide to successful environmental training*

'Ann's book is about women who are still doing the things they've always done and for which historically, they've often been scorned and even overmedicated for doing. This is a book about women seeing modern day problems and acting to address them by offering sanctuary and solace to those in need. It's a book about women courageously speaking up in heroic ways regardless of the consequences. During her stories, we meet ordinary women who choose not to sit on the sidelines whilst watching all manner of inequality. *Women Behaving Courageously* is a timely discourse about brave women rising to challenge the status quo and how they are succeeding against all the odds by lighting a path to a better future in a 'woman's way'.'

Kay Urlich
Author of *The Metamorphosis of Humanity: THE FEMALE EFFECT*

'Before reading Ann's book I thought I was reasonably well informed – I stand corrected. There was much about the evolution of women's rights I was oblivious to. What an enlightening, provocative and incredible 'can't-put-it-down' read. I've come away feeling educated, empowered, and more committed to action. Ann, thank you for your relentless commitment to saying what needs to be said. I am in awe of you, always.'

Simonne Liley
The Accountant's Coach

Dedicated to my beautiful granddaughters:

Tayla, Ella and Casey

and to their granddaughters and their granddaughters

INTRODUCTION

As an avid reader and an even more avid writer, I'm always fascinated by the ideas that trigger a book. I was chatting to a lovely young neighbour over the Christmas break and she mentioned that she had been in 'Gladys Aylward House' during her school days. I was able to tell her that I'd actually been within feet of Gladys Aylward many years before.

I was living in Gosport, England during my service in the Women's Royal Navy and every day I would see this tiny woman walking along our street with a group of unusual-looking children. This was during the 1960s, long before immigration, so I'd only ever known white Anglo-Saxons. I watched in absolute wonder as this happy group passed my window every day. I learned from a neighbour that she was Gladys Aylward, and the children were Chinese. I found out later that Aylward was the heroine of a book and a movie and here she was passing by my home, right here in front of me, in real life.

In those days we didn't have the Google search engine, so I headed to a local library to find out more about this amazing little woman. It turns out that in 1939 she was working as a maid when she had a vision or a 'calling'. Her call was to go to China as a missionary. Imagine that. Alan Burgess wrote the book *The Small Woman* on which the movie *The Inn of the Sixth Happiness* was based.

Needless to say her efforts to get to China were met with roadblocks and derision at every turn. She was a maid; she had no training as a missionary; she couldn't speak Chinese. How dare she think she was being 'called'? Eventually, after writing repeatedly to the China Inland Mission and being declined again and again, she finally found a saviour in Sir Francis Jamison who wrote on her behalf to a colleague of his, Jeannie Lawson, who ran an inn in China. The inn was a Christian organisation that provided cheap food and Bible studies to locals and travellers, with the hope of spreading Christianity.

The inn was actually called 'The Inn of the Eight Happinesses'. The 'happinesses' are based on eight virtues: love, virtue, gentleness, tolerance, loyalty, truth, beauty and devotion.

Aylward eventually made the arduous trip and joined Mrs Lawson. Sadly, after only a very short period of time, Mrs Lawson had a serious accident and was forced to close the doors on the inn. The local mandarin saw an opportunity to persuade a British woman (Gladys) to assist him to implement a government decree to end the hideous practice of binding women's feet. She agreed to do the job on condition that she could reopen the inn and keep offering their Christian services.

Eventually Aylward became a Chinese citizen and a fluent Chinese speaker. She was beloved by the locals for adopting abandoned children and caring for them in her inn. The locals even gave her the Chinese name 'Jennai'. Literally translated this means 'the one who loves people', in honour of the good work she did for them.

Years passed and rumours of a Japanese invasion started to alarm everyone. Aylward accompanied an army colonel around the many villages to alert people and instruct them in how to prepare themselves for war. As she visited the various villages, she gathered up even more orphaned children and took them into her care, realising that this had been her calling all along; to save the children.

In 1938 the region was indeed invaded by the Japanese. Aylward led more than 100 children, some as young as two and three, over a massive mountain range in the middle of winter. During this dangerous trek, to lift their spirits and to keep them moving she taught the children the song 'This Old Man' ('... with a knick-knack paddywhack, give a dog a bone, this old man came rolling home'). I've recently learned that Gladys Aylward, this truly remarkable woman, ended her days running an orphanage in Taiwan. A befitting final chapter in her wonderful life and story.

Chatting about Gladys Aylward moved me to thinking about other courageous women who had in some way inspired me in my own life.

From about four years old I'd wanted to become a nurse, so stories of Florence Nightingale and Edith Cavell were the women that delighted and encouraged me.

Florence Nightingale was born in 1820 to a middle-class family and became a nurse despite her parents' vehement objections. At that time nursing was not seen as a job for gentlewomen. Undeterred she became a nurse and literally changed the face of nursing from being perceived as the lowest of low occupations into a highly skilled and respected profession. Her fame as 'the lady with the lamp' evolved out of her care and devotion as she visited soldiers at night; soldiers who had been terribly wounded in the Crimean War, some of whom would die from their injuries.

Edith Cavell was my second nursing inspiration. Although British, Cavell started her working life as a governess for a Belgian family. Her father became seriously ill in England and so she returned home to look after him. This was her first introduction to nursing and a career she felt destined to follow.

While she was going through her nursing training, the First World War broke out. As a Belgian-speaking nurse she felt the need to move back to Belgium to do her part in the war effort. Even though Britain and Europe were at war with Germany, she made it clear that her nurses would treat *all* soldiers who were brought to their hospital regardless of nationality.

In 1914, German advances into Belgium left her and her patients vulnerable. She decided to help British, Belgian and French soldiers escape to Holland (the Netherlands) via an underground network of tunnels. Holland had remained neutral during the war and so the country was able to give injured soldiers sanctuary and a stop-off point before making their way back home. She aided their escape with a small amount of money, fake identity cards and secret passwords for their safe passage.

A Belgian spy discovered the secret tunnel beneath the hospital and reported it to German authorities. Cavell was arrested and interrogated by German officials. Because she chose not to lie, she confessed to having helped soldiers escape and tragically on 12 October 1915, Edith Cavell was executed by a German firing squad despite outrage and pleas for mercy from all over the world.

All this reflection of historical female heroes had me pondering modern-day women and their role in a furiously changing society. As we begin the second decade of 2000, the world is facing all manner of challenges: an ever-growing population; how to feed 7.5 billion people; how to gainfully employ this sheer mass of people given the advent of robotics. We are witnessing whole species of wildlife being decimated because of habitat destruction, the burning of rainforests to make way for farming, seas being over-fished and polluted with plastic, not to mention the very real signs of a rapidly warming planet. And if all these situations weren't terrifying enough, being hit with the Covid-19 pandemic at the start of 2020 which resulted in hundreds of thousands of deaths across the world surely has to be taken as a wake-up call.

If we are to survive, if we are to feed ourselves, if we are to halt the mass extinction of species and if we are to ensure the planet doesn't burn itself into oblivion and wipe out the human race, then I firmly believe that over the next decade the world will see a massive shift in values.

I also firmly believe the values that will save the planet will be female driven.

We can no longer keep up this quest for more and more, whether that is for more and more land, or more and more power, or more and more wealth. Gandhi famously said: 'The earth has enough for man's needs but not enough for his greed.'

This book isn't about trashing men or blaming them for where the world is right now. I have a gorgeous husband, a fabulous son and three divine grandsons, but 'drive' is a male tendency; success and winning is what motivates our darling men. The problem is, though, that this quest for more and more and more is literally costing the earth.

So I started thinking about the women of courage of the last few decades who were and are saying loudly and categorically 'ENOUGH!'.

Enough of the power grabs; enough of a few people being fabulously wealthy while millions can barely make ends meet, even with several jobs. Enough of the dog-eat-dog ways of the last few thousand years; enough of wiping out species; enough of exploiting women and children; and absolutely enough of damaging the only planet we have.

> *'It took me quite a long time to develop a voice, and now that I have it, I am not going to be silent.'*
>
> *Madeleine Albright*

OUTLINE OF THE BOOK

In Chapter 1 I investigate how previous generations of women have shaped the world. I delve into what our mothers, grandmothers and in some cases even great-grandmothers taught us about being a woman. Because the book was intended to be about 'warrior women', I felt the need to explore the difference between a hero and a warrior. I researched the suffragette movement; I discovered that some of the women in that movement were deliberately and unapologetically militant while others were not. I look at countries where, even in 2020, some women still don't have the right to vote, or voting is made so dangerous that women simply don't bother.

Chapter 2 is given over to 25 'warrior women'. I've selected women who are taking on the modern male-dominated world in their own way. Like the suffragettes, some are loud and deliberate, while others choose a quieter way without sacrificing a determination to make a difference. Some are fighting to make the world a safer and more equal world for girls and women, others are doing their best to save the planet.

In Chapter 3 I discuss the ways men set up society as it is today. I look at paternalism; what it is, why it is so offensive to women, and why women standing up to a paternalistic society is giving some men the vapours. I look at the effect of paternalism on women's reproductive rights. I explore why some older white men are angry at the changes going on around them, while other men are unashamedly supporting women's rights to equal pay and an equal voice.

Chapter 4 is dedicated to understanding feminism. What it is, how it came about; why some men hate the word and why some women refuse to be classed as a feminist. I highlight how young women differ from previous generations; how they are angry yet have no fear of vocalising their anger.

In Chapter 5 I show the myriad of ways greed is destroying so many aspects of our society; the strain it is putting on the environment and the long-term damage being done to species. I explore when and where we seemed to lose the plot; when the gap between rich and poor first started to widen so we now have some CEOs earning more in an hour than some workers earn in an entire year. I investigate the ways corporates are now being reined in, knowing that their quest for more and more profits really is costing the earth.

In Chapter 6 I share stories of the millions of women who are making waves and saying 'Enough!'. I highlight some of the work being done via the annual International Women's Day conferences. At the 2019 conference, women from the Solomon Islands, Cambodia, Fiji and Chile spoke about the powerful work they were doing to improve the lives of women and girls in their various countries. I discuss the value of values and how they got lost somewhere along the way in exchange for never-ending profits. I tell the story of Icelandic women who, after their country's financial crisis, took over all key banking positions. These women now teach others how to set up and run their businesses on the basis of female values.

Finally, I ask what would happen in society and business if, before we made a decision, we asked the question, 'What would kindness do?'

Chapter 7 is about fulfilling your destiny; it explores your life path. I show the reader where some of the most powerful women in the world fit in terms of their 'calling'. I discuss why some women have chosen to work from the power of good, while others with the same life path have made darker choices.

Chapter 8, my final chapter, introduces the reader to the idea that we're never too old and it's never too late to make a difference. I share a fictional story of small groups of women who took on virtually every aspect of society and changed society for the better, one project at a time. I explain how seven different groups saw an opportunity to do something, and just got on and did it. I ask what the world needs to do differently to make sure our grandchildren actually have a future, and I ask the reader what she will do differently as a result of having read this book.

> *'Educate a man and you educate a man; educate a woman and you educate a whole nation.'*
>
> *Dr James Emman Kwegyir Aggrey*

1

HOW WOMEN HAVE ALREADY SHAPED THE WORLD

'It's called civilisation. Women invented it and every time we men blow it to bits, they just invent it again.'

Orson Scott Card

The difference between a hero and a warrior

As I was thinking about brave women, I thought about all the women I know who 'just get on with things'. No fuss, no mess, no drama. We may not class them as warriors, but for sure they are heroes.

Definitions: a hero is a real or mythical person of great bravery who carries out extraordinary deeds; a warrior is a person who is actively engaged in battle, conflict or warfare, a soldier or combatant.

My grandparents opted to bring me up, an illegitimate child in a small town where everyone knew I was illegitimate at a time when illegitimacy was not a cause for celebration. They never questioned their decision to raise me when it would have been so easy for them to insist that I be put up for adoption. They were heroes.

Think of women who have to give up a promising career to take care of a sick or handicapped child. Women who walk away from a career to care for elderly parents. Think of grandparents who instead of putting their feet up in their golden years take over raising grandchildren because their adult children can't or won't look after *their* children. These people are heroes.

Think about people, male or female, who are diagnosed with terminal illnesses; people who survive horrific accidents or come back from war zones mentally and physically broken. Think about people who lose a child or partner; think about people who suffer from depression. For all these people, simply getting out of bed in the morning and putting two feet on the floor ready to face another tough day makes them *all* heroes.

If you have chosen to stay home with a handicapped child and give up your career, you are blessed. If you have chosen to walk away from a fabulous income to devote yourself to looking after an elderly parent, you are truly a hero, and if you have experienced some kind of horrendous loss and you are still getting on with things, one day at a time, then all hail you.

> *'One thing I just want to say to the military families: while you might not wear a uniform, I know, we all know, the nation knows, that you serve and sacrifice right alongside your loved ones. And we are so grateful and proud of all of you for your service to this nation.'*
>
> *Michelle Obama*

What our mothers, grandmothers and even great-grandmothers taught us

My grandmother was a hero even before she chose to raise me.

She was the oldest of four daughters. When she was 12 years old her mother died so she had to leave school and basically take over her mother's role, feeding, washing and cleaning for her father and three younger sisters. My grandmother survived the Great Depression and two world wars. She also survived breast cancer. I actually never heard her complain ever; about anything. She just got on with things, doing the things that grandmothers and mothers do during tough times. She made a home, looked after her family and learned to make everything stretch.

I once heard the amazing stories of two Nobel Prize winners who were asked how their mothers had shaped their lives. One said that when he came home from school every day, his mother wouldn't ask if he'd had a good day at school, she would ask, 'What great questions did you ask today?' The second winner said that his family had also survived the Great Depression when food was extremely scarce and that they had lived on leftovers — he joked that they had never ever found the original meal.

My mother worked in a munitions factory at the beginning of the Second World War, eventually joining the Women's Royal Navy where she served until the end of that war. All the male members of my family fought in some way during the war. This left my grandmother, my mother and her younger sister to fare as best they could with the shortage of food and clothing, blackouts, lack of fuel in extremely cold winters; a scarcity of even the barest of necessities. They too just got on with it.

There were no career aspirations for my grandmother's generation, there was none for my mother's generation and, sadly, my generation didn't get a great deal of encouragement either. For our three generations, it was a case of get a job, any sort of job until you marry.

Once they married, both my mother and grandmother were expected to leave the workplace; in my generation we were expected to leave the workplace once we reached the six-month mark of our first pregnancy. We were encouraged into one of three occupations: nursing, teaching or secretarial work, the premise being that once our children were older, we could return to work and these positions allowed more flexibility with school holidays.

I had a particularly unpleasant 'home' situation, so I gave up on the dream of being a nurse and chose the fast-track career of becoming a secretary. I took a one-year senior secretarial course at Scarborough Technical College, then applied for and was accepted into the Women's Royal Navy thereby following in my mother's footsteps. If I had chosen the nursing route I would have had to stay at home during my training. There was no way I felt safe doing that.

For two generations once these women left the workplace, they were finished career wise. Not much had changed for my generation; we were not encouraged or even advised to think too loftily. Even in my day, often workplaces wouldn't hire women at all, the fear being that once they got married they would be useless, so why bother hiring them and training them only to watch them leave?

Because I couldn't get a job when my children were small, I became a Tupperware lady. I did this work so that my husband could look after our children in the evenings and we were then able to earn a bit of extra money to pay for a few luxuries. We're not talking the 1800s here, we're talking the 1970s. The Tupperware company policy at that time was that if a woman became successful at selling their products and reached a certain sales target, her husband would be invited into the business to manage her!

When I first came to New Zealand with my then husband and small children, I wanted to be able to purchase clothing at our local Farmers store. To be able to do that, I was given a form to complete that was to be signed by my husband giving me permission to open an account in *his* name!

So for generations men have been the 'breadwinners'; the head of the household, the decision-makers. Early censuses reflect that status. In the 1700s and 1800s it was probably how it had to be. Women had no form of birth control and so large families were the norm. Women had neither the education, the time nor, I would imagine, the energy to do anything other than look after children.

In many Third World countries, educating girls is still seen as a waste of time and money.

> *'I was not supposed to be in any way a liberated person. I was a female born in the 1940s in a patriarchal family; I was supposed to marry and make everyone around me happy.'*
>
> *Isabel Allende*

The suffragettes

Since the mid-1800s women in Britain had been agitating to be given the right to vote in general elections. Emmeline Pankhurst was the activist who spent 40 years trying to achieve what the women before her had failed to do. The women who joined her movement were often imprisoned; frequently force fed and abused verbally, physically and mentally for their efforts.

Make no mistake, the suffragettes were deliberately loud and sensational. They were very deliberately militant. They attacked property, chained themselves to railings and generally disrupted society in ways never previously seen, particularly by women. The suffragettes felt it had already taken way too long and that previous efforts had been too ladylike, genteel and slow. No wishy-washy tameness for them.

One of the leaders of the group — Emily Davison — was arrested on nine occasions, went on hunger strike seven times and was force fed on 49 occasions. She literally threw herself in front of King George V's horse at the Epsom Derby and subsequently died of her injuries. She became a martyr for the cause.

A women's rights convention held in Seneca Falls, New York in 1848 is credited with being the event that launched the suffragette movement in America, yet it took until 1920 for them to be finally given the right to vote.

Women in New Zealand were given the vote on 19 September 1893, the first country in the world to accord that right to women. It took until 1928 for women in Britain to be given the vote, and until 1971 for the women of Switzerland; women in Lichtenstein had to wait until 1984.

Even though the efforts to win the right to vote in the UK had been slow, some women didn't agree with these tactics. They believed it fed into the already entrenched belief by the men of the day that because women menstruated, they were way too emotional to be trusted with a vote, that their place literally was in the home. The same rationale was used to keep women out of university and out of the professions. Men felt that all this emotion once per month meant women were simply too unstable to be trusted with a vote or position of responsibility.

For thousands of years we women have been labelled 'emotional'. 'Hysteria was the first mental disorder attributed to women (and only women). It was an all-embracing, catch-all diagnosis for symptoms including nervousness, hallucinations, emotional outbursts and various urges of the sexual variety.'

In a hilarious article by Catherine Pearson, 'Female Hysteria: 7 Crazy Things People Used to Believe about the Ladies' Disease', she writes that it was thought to be caused by 'wandering wombs, sexy thoughts and that it could be cured by pelvic massage, a vibrator or a good hosing down'.

Really funny on one level, but incredibly sad on another when you wonder if we've travelled very far from that level of thinking.

I recently had a skin complaint; an itch at the back of my neck that had no obvious signs of an infection or irritation. The male skin specialist I was referred to told me that in the 1950s if a woman presented with an 'itch' and there was no visible cause, they were diagnosed as being nymphomaniacs! At this suggestion, the female nurse and I made eye contact and both of us rolled our eyes. I eventually worked out that the cause of the itch was something in the clothing labels the manufacturers used.

> *'Men make the moral code and they expect women to accept it. They have decided that it is entirely right and proper for men to fight for their liberties and their rights, but that it is not right and proper for women to fight for theirs.'*
>
> *Emmeline Pankhurst*

Rosie the Riveter

Eleanor Roosevelt, wife of President Roosevelt, had been so impressed by British women taking over all manner of male roles during the Second World War in the UK that in 1941 she was instrumental in doing the same for American women by launching the famous 'Rosie the Riveter' campaign.

My mum was a British equivalent of Rosie the Riveter, working in that munitions factory doing her bit for the British war effort. Women were brought into such work for the first time in history so able-bodied men could be freed to fight in the various armed forces during the Second World War; during the First World War women had been allowed to drive ambulances and roll bandages.

So because of the Second World War, in America and Britain women entered the workforce in record numbers. By 1945 virtually one in every four married women worked outside the home; something that had previously been impossible because of the custom of women being forced to leave the workplace once they married.

Germany would probably have won the war if not for these women, yet despite the dangerous work they were now doing, they still earned only half of a man's wage for doing the same job.

Calling on women to take over traditional male roles was only meant to be a temporary initiative. It was fully expected that once men returned from fighting, women would return to being housewives. For many women this caused fury.

By stepping in and taking over virtually every job previously done by men, women believed that they had proven that they were just as intelligent, just as capable and just as hard-working as any man.

They had enjoyed the stimulation of the workplace and had

discovered the luxury of earning their own money. The Second World War changed the workplace for ever and it gave women a freedom they had never previously experienced. It was not going to be given up lightly. They were not about to be told to 'get back into the kitchen'.

> *'For all the men who say that a woman's place is in the kitchen, they need to remember that is where the knives are kept.'*
>
> *Not known*

Countries where women still don't have the right to vote

The Vatican absolutely refuses to give women the right to vote. Saudi Arabia finally allowed women the vote in 2015, and women have been given 'access to education without the consent of a father, a brother, husband or uncle'.

In Afghanistan and under Shi'a law, women still must ask permission to leave the house. Before the Taliban, Afghani women had had the vote since 1964. In 2014, Afghani women came out in record numbers to vote and even run for office despite threats of violence and even death from the Taliban. Pakistani women can be banned from voting by their husbands and community elders. Those who courageously step out to cast a vote still face harassment, despite the segregated voting booths.

In the 2016 elections in Uganda, violence against women trying to vote was so extreme that control centres were set up to protect them. Also, however, deliberate delays were set up so the women were discouraged from waiting in line, knowing they had so many domestic chores waiting for them at home.

In Kenya, distances to polling booths and the threats of violence along the way similarly discourage women from voting. In western Kenya, pregnant women are forbidden to be seen in public so they too are prevented from their voting rights. In north-eastern Kenya, societal conflict means women are discouraged from walking the long distances to registration centres, not to mention the physical insecurity of being out alone for a long period of time.

It wasn't until 2003 that women in Oman were given voting rights. They are actually told what to vote by their husbands and risk being divorced if they refuse to vote the way their husbands tell them to.

Egypt has been nominated as the worst country in the Arab world for women's rights even though women have had the right to vote since 1956. In 2015, Egyptian women were banned for voting in 'revealing attire' but were given the double burden of having to remove their niqab veil to be identified. The law prevents women from showing their faces in public, so they are damned if they do and damned if they don't.

Nigerian women do have the right to vote, but don't feel their vote counts. Their president, Muhammadu Buhari, while on a visit to Germany, claimed publicly that 'I don't know which party my wife belongs to, but she belongs to my kitchen and my living room and the other room.' He said this while standing at the side of Angela Merkel, three times Chancellor of Germany.

Suppression of women goes on in countries all over the world despite over 200 years of women fighting for their rights. On a good day it seems that women are finally making progress; on a bad day it would seem that at best we are standing still, at worst it may feel that we are going backwards.

And we must not let that happen.

> *'Religion is against women's rights and women's freedom. In all societies women are oppressed by all religions.'*
>
> *Taslima Nasrin*

Questions regarding the introduction and Chapter 1

What has surprised you so far?

What has upset you so far?

What has shocked you so far?

Which of the happiness 'virtues' stood out for you?

In what ways have you already been a hero?

Do you think you might possibly have a 'calling'?

If so, what have you done about that to date?

2

THERE'S WORK TO BE DONE AND WOMEN WILL DO IT

'I will never accept life for what it is. I don't need an easy life. My road was meant to be hard because anything worth having in this world will take me to the very edge of myself. I will overcome everything I have ever gone through and will make my future the one God intended me to have. I will pick up the pieces of this pain and sculpt it into art. I am not ordinary and never was. I walk into my birth right as a queen with her head held high. I was born to do this!'

Shannon L. Alder

Warriors come in many shapes and sizes

The quiet warriors

Dame Jane Goodall

Dame Jane Goodall is one of the quiet warriors. These women don't rage and shout or stand on soapboxes; they just quietly go about their business, making their case, standing their ground and doing what they believe they are on this earth to do.

Goodall was given a stuffed chimpanzee as a child instead of a doll or a teddy. She has always been passionate about animals and was fortunate enough to spend time on a farm in Kenya as a young woman.

She had no formal training in working with animals, but she had her eye on getting a secretarial job with Louis Leakey, a renowned archaeologist and palaeontologist. She had no aspirations to work with the animals, she just wanted to be alongside someone who did work with animals. Leakey was interested in studying apes and chimps in more depth and so he sent Jane to study primate behaviour at the University of Cambridge, and the rest is history.

Goodall has now spent 55 years studying and sharing her knowledge of primates with the world, in particular her fear that their habitats are being decimated and their survival is in doubt.

She was once asked if she believed in God and she replied: 'I have no idea who or what God is, but I do believe in some great spiritual power. I feel it when I'm out in nature. It's just something that's bigger and stronger than what I am or what anybody is. I feel it. And it's enough for me.'

'Do something outside of yourself that you really care about, that

you are passionate about, whether it's the environment [or] discrimination. Do something that will make life a little better for people less fortunate than you.'

Dame Jane Goodall

Ruth Bader Ginsburg

Ginsburg is another quiet warrior: she is one of the few women on the American Supreme Court, a position she has held for 26 years after being appointed by President Clinton. She graduated first in her Cornell University class, went on to attend Harvard Law School and was one of only nine women in a class of 500 students. And despite such a stellar background, she still faced workplace discrimination.

A staunch advocate of women's rights and gender equality, Ginsburg has a quiet and dignified style of getting her points across. She has stated quite clearly that 'reacting in anger or annoyance will not advance one's ability to persuade.' Her style has drawn praise and respect from all sides of the American political divide.

Now 87 years old and experiencing various health challenges, Ginsburg is an eternal optimist. She particularly loves the fact that over the past few years, young people have become fired up and that they are fighting to make America the country they want it to be.

She classes herself as a gender equality champion and says that being a mother during the '70s when the second wave of feminism took the world by storm was for her 'a tremendous stroke of fortune'. She acknowledges that women haven't reached nirvana, but that women have travelled a massive way from the days when they couldn't do things just because they were female.

She admits to being particularly enamoured and encouraged by Malala Yousafzai and Greta Thunberg, 'two wonderful women not yet twenty years old who both in their different ways have taken the world by storm'.

'You can disagree without being disagreeable.'

Ruth Bader Ginsburg

The gracious warriors

Christine Blasey Ford

Ford is an American professor of psychology at Palo Alto University; she was also a research psychologist at Stanford University.

In July 2018 she heard that Brett Kavanaugh was on the shortlist to become Associate Justice of the Supreme Court of the United States. She immediately contacted the *Washington Post* and her congresswoman Anna Eshoo and told the story of sexual abuse by Kavanaugh when they were in college. She asked for confidentiality. Her aim was that someone should know that Kavanaugh was not a credible person to be offered such a powerful position: a lifetime tenure in the Supreme Court.

In September 2018 she stepped into the glaring global spotlight to give details of her abuse. She spoke with calm dignity, told her story, endured an invasive cross-examination and stood her ground. Not once did she lose her cool, not once did she become emotional and at no stage did she become irrational.

An FBI investigation was ordered yet dozens of witnesses who were at the party in question were never interviewed. Kavanaugh, who during his cross-examination had been decidedly emotional, angry, volatile and at times incoherent, was confirmed into a lifelong appointment on 6 October 2018.

Meanwhile, Ford received hate male and death threats that were so concerning, she and her family were forced to move out of their family home and she was no longer able to continue in her professional role. Even months later she was still receiving abusive threats and had moved home four times.

Someone was so incensed by her treatment that they set up a GoFundMe account for her. At the time of closing the account, US$647,610 had been amassed. Ford used some of the money to pay for security for herself and her family, and planned to donate the balance to trauma survivors.

In November 2019, she was awarded the ACLU of Southern California's Roger Baldwin Courage Award for speaking out against Kavanaugh.

> *'Thousands of people who have had their lives dramatically altered by sexual violence have reached out to share their own experiences with me and have thanked me for coming forward. At the same time, my greatest fears have been realized—and the reality has been far worse than what I expected. My family and I have been the target of constant harassment and death threats. I have been called the most vile and hateful names imaginable. These messages, while far fewer than the expressions of support, have been terrifying to receive and have rocked me to my core.'*
>
> *Christine Blasey Ford*

Michelle Obama

Michelle Obama was raised in a household that valued education. Michelle and her brother were both able to read by age four. By sixth grade, Michelle was placed in a gifted programme, which led to her attending Whitney M. Young Magnet High School, Chicago's first school for gifted children. She went on to attend Princeton University and from there to Harvard Law School. This is where her form of militancy began, taking part in demonstrations calling for the enrolment of more minority students and professors.

Michelle became the associate dean of student services at the

University of Chicago and developed the university's first ever community service programme. This led to her being employed as executive director of community relations and external affairs for the University of Chicago Medical Center.

After meeting Barack Obama and being asked to make speeches as he started on the campaign trail, it was clear that she was a natural orator. One person in one of Barack's audiences had said, 'You are great, Barack, but your wife, she is something else!'

Being the mother of two daughters, Michelle became vocal and passionate about protecting women from sexual harassment and encouraging schools and families to teach their girls to speak up if they were feeling uncomfortable or unsafe. She believed that girls should be taught the power of saying 'No' or 'Don't touch me' so that from a very early age as they grew into young women, their confidence was inbuilt.

As the first black family to move into the White House, they were subject to a particularly vengeful form of bullying from a part of the country that still hadn't come to terms with an integrated society. No matter how many insults were flung her way or Barack's way, her reaction was always 'They go low, we go high'.

During her eight years as America's first lady, Michelle Obama paid for her entire wardrobe, including designer clothes, out of her own pocket.

> *'I wake up every morning in a house that was built by slaves, and I watch my daughters, two beautiful, intelligent, black young women, playing with their dogs on the White House lawn, and because of Hillary Clinton, my daughters, and all our sons and daughters, now take for granted that a woman can be president of the United States.'*
>
> *Michelle Obama*

Jacinda Ardern

Ardern is the third female prime minister of New Zealand. When she became prime minister she was just 37 years old and the world's youngest head of government.

We saw a first-hand example of her grace under fire here in New Zealand on 15 March 2019. An Australian white supremacist raided the Al Noor Mosque in Christchurch firing at will with a semi-automatic assault weapon. He then drove to the Islamic Centre a short distance away and opened fire on even more people who were simply at prayer. Fifty-one people were killed and a further 49 were seriously injured. He was subsequently charged with 51 murders, 40 attempted murders and engaging in a terrorist act.

Ardern acted immediately. There was no instruction manual for what to do in the event of a massacre. In our history there has been only one other mass shooting and this happened in 1990 when Ardern was just 10 years old.

Ardern made a public announcement immediately. She acknowledged that this was one of New Zealand's darkest days, going on to say 'many of the victims chose to make New Zealand their home and they should have felt safe. There is no place in New Zealand for such acts of extreme and unprecedented violence.'

Her calm and dignified leadership at a moment of the most extreme terror New Zealand had ever witnessed reassured us all. Her famous 'They are us' comment led to an outpouring of help and care for Muslim communities throughout New Zealand as they dealt with the horror, the shock and the grief. She banned the gunman's name from ever being mentioned in New Zealand — she simply refused to recognise him as a person.

One of the most gut-wrenching aspects of what he did was the fact that as he was gunning people down, he was videoing his actions and live-streaming the videos on Facebook. Facebook was alerted by the New Zealand police that a live massacre was being streamed. It took Facebook over half an hour to shut the video down, by which time it had gone out to over 1.5 million viewers and was subsequently shared to millions more via YouTube, Twitter, Facebook and Reddit.

Here in New Zealand, anyone downloading, watching or sharing the video is immediately prosecuted.

Less than one month after the massacre, our politicians voted en masse to ban semi-automatic and military-style weapons. Owners of such guns were given a deadline to hand in their guns and be paid the market rate for them. Anyone found holding on to such weapons faces up to five years in prison.

She tackled Facebook and spoke directly with Sheryl Sandberg, Facebook's COO. In a speech to Parliament later that same day she said that she would stand up to Facebook and absolutely demand change. She was emphatic that 'We cannot simply sit back and accept that these platforms just exist and that what is said on them is not the responsibility of the place where they are published. They are the publisher. Not just the postman.'

Support for her actions came from all over the world. Australia's prime minister, Scott Morrison, called for 'a social media crackdown in the wake of the attacks'. He then wrote to the G20 chairman, Japanese prime minister Shinzo Abe, asking that social media reform be top priority at the next G20 meeting. Two months after the massacre, Ardern was in France working with President Macron of France and the G7 leaders as they developed a joint strategy for dealing with the giant tech companies going forward to ensure they took some responsibility for what people were uploading.

Their pledge is known as the Christchurch Call and is a promise to tackle terrorist and extreme violence that appears online.

Leaders of major internet companies Google, Facebook, Microsoft and Twitter were at the meeting. The USA refused to sign the agreement, stating that it hindered freedom of speech, and Mark Zuckerberg, founder and CEO of Facebook, did not attend.

As a result of her swift response to the massacre and her humane reaction to the Muslim communities affected, *Fortune* magazine acknowledged her as the second greatest leader for the year, second only to Bill and Melinda Gates, who work tirelessly fighting health crises around the world.

The sad thing for Ardern is that even though outside of New Zealand she is revered, within New Zealand she takes a battering from people who did not like what she did on that day and do not like what she stands for. Ardern is head of the New Zealand Labour Party. She came into power after nine years of a conservative government where their policy seemed to be sell everything that wasn't nailed down, creating what was proclaimed throughout the Western world as a rock star economy. House and land prices went through the roof as overseas buyers bought up pristine coastline and properties in popular suburbs. Often these houses were left empty. For overseas investors it was just that, an investment. However, the outcome was that ordinary New Zealanders were priced out of the market.

One of her first moves when she came into power was to stop sales to overseas buyers who did not actually reside in the country. Ardern puts people before the economy, which for some seems to be unforgiveable.

She was also berated for wearing a headscarf to meetings with the grieving Muslim families and with the wider Muslim community. Some people felt she was minimising women by doing that. I'm pretty sure that no matter which community had suffered at the hands of a terrorist, she would have worn whatever clothing was appropriate for that particular community as they grieved, whether they were Jewish, Roman Catholic, Hindu or whatever. She was simply showing respect.

Fortunately, for every person who decries her, there are thousands of us who love and support her humanity. We hope that she never lets such people grind her down or change her in any way. She was absolutely the right person to lead us at such a horrifying time and in exactly the right way.

> *'We were not chosen for this act of violence because we condone racism, because we are an enclave for extremism. We were chosen for the very fact that we are none of those things.'*
>
> *Jacinda Ardern*

The business warriors

Dame Anita Roddick

Roddick surely rocked the business world when she opened her first Body Shop in 1976. Her determination was that her products would be clean, green and *not* tested on animals. She trekked around numerous banks with a baby on her hip to apply for her first business loan and was repeatedly turned away. She was only able to open her first shop when her husband loaned her four thousand pounds. It's a sad indictment that she had to borrow from her husband; wasn't that 'their' money?

Roddick's differed from traditional beauty products in that she never claimed her products would stave off wrinkles or old age. Long before Fair Trade was even heard of, she sourced directly from ground-level growers, was anti-packaging and promoted the 'self-return and refill' purpose of her very unsexy bottles.

As more shops opened she recruited staff on the premise that every employee would spend one day a month doing community work, something that eventually banks emulated. The very banks that had turned her away!

She pioneered the green beauty movement. All her shops had a socially aware project on the go where people were encouraged to sign up and become part of making the world a better place — all of which seemed quite bonkers in the greedy self-centred times of the '80s.

By the 1990s she was the fourth-richest woman in Britain and was a regular and generous contributor to many pacifist, ecological and human rights causes.

This amazing lady died on 10 September 2007 of a brain haemorrhage after suffering from hepatitis C for over 30 years. She was just 64 years old. What a loss.

> *'I love her like fury, but it's like being trapped in a brown paper bag with a bluebottle. Like all true entrepreneurs, she fired on all cylinders, all the time. Working close to her would have driven me mad, but working alongside her in an extraordinary nexus of ethical, social, environmental and international development movements has been one of the great privileges of my life.'*
>
> *John Elkington*

Melinda Gates

Melinda Gates had an early interest in computers. While taking an advanced math class at the Ursuline Academy, she went on to follow her computer interest in college and earned a bachelor's degree in computer sciences from Duke University.

She took a job at Microsoft and eventually married the boss, Bill Gates. The same year she and Bill married they co-founded what was to become the Bill & Melinda Gates Foundation. Their philanthropy has been nothing less than staggering. Initially they had planned to put computers into libraries all over America so that everyone had access to a computer. Over the years Melinda broadened that vision to encompass global improvements in education, poverty and health issues.

Their foundation was massively boosted in 2006 when investor Warren Buffett donated US$30 billion, the largest amount ever donated to a charity. This allowed the foundation to develop strategies for prevention of HIV/AIDS, malaria and tuberculosis far more rapidly than they had dreamed possible.

Microsoft itself is leading the way as a progressive workplace. In 2015 they announced that employees of their foundation could take one year's leave after the birth or adoption of a child.

In 2012 Melinda pledged US$560 million towards improving access to contraception for women in poor countries, and is investing US$1 billion over 10 years to expanding women's power and influence in the American workforce. She admits to outrage when she discovered that even in 2018, there were more men called 'James' running Fortune 500 companies than there were women. Just 24 women run Fortune 500 companies.

In 2016 the Gates' work was recognised by President Barack Obama when they were presented with the Presidential Medal of Freedom.

Melinda continues her work for women and the under-represented. She confesses to have been overjoyed when hundreds of thousands of women marched across the country post Trump moving into the Oval Office. She applauded the enormous courage of the #MeToo movement as women came forward and told their stories. She was delighted at the record number of women who ran for and succeeded in winning seats in the 2018 US mid-term elections.

Her greatest fear is that all that passion will dissipate; that the media will grow tired of reporting on inequality and that diversity will remain something that corporates talk about, pay lip service to, or do nothing about. That 'all of this energy and attention has amounted to a temporary swell instead of a sea change'.

> *'To the women who are working multiple jobs, caring for multiple loved ones, and proving you don't have to protest or enter politics to challenge a system stacked against you. It wasn't just grand gestures that got us here. It was daily acts of courage, too.'*
>
> *Melinda Gates*

The unintentional warriors

Linda Ronstadt

Ronstadt was born and raised on a 10-acre ranch in Tucson, Arizona. Her father was a wealthy machinery merchant and her mother was the daughter of Lloyd Groff Copeman, famous inventor and holder of 700 patents. He is credited with developing the early toaster, the first electric stove and an early form of the microwave oven.

Ronstadt has had a prolific singing career and amassed numerous awards, but as she got older, she was diagnosed with a degenerative form of palsy that was already affecting her throat and ability to sing.

The reason I've included her in this story of warrior women isn't that she has been a prolific activist; she has actually had a fairly behind-the-scenes life and career, however, at some moment in time when an opportunity occurs for any of us, she is the living example of literally 'finding your voice and seizing the moment'.

Ronstadt was attending an event where she and Sally Field were being honoured. After the event she said that she had had no intention of mentioning Trump or saying anything about the current administration, however, during her acceptance speech she said that, in her opinion, we were now living in an era when the idea of truth was being challenged.

Half the audience applauded, half the audience stayed silent.

Mike Pompeo was a guest speaker at the event and very dangerously asked, 'When will I be loved?', a reference to a Ronstadt hit. Her response from the stage: 'When you stop enabling Trump.'

Kapow!

Ronstadt's moment of truth.

> *'We wanted to sing about the passions of mature women: love and concern for our children, love between trusted and treasured friends, the precariousness of romantic love, the difference between the love you give to the living and the love you give to the dead, the bitterness of a lost love remembered, and the long, steady love you keep for good.'*
>
> *Linda Ronstadt, Simple Dreams: A musical memoir*

Elissa Slotkin

Slotkin is possibly a warrior you've never heard of. She is a former CIA analyst and little-known Democratic senator who was one of that tidal wave of women who stepped forward and won selection in the 2018 American mid-term elections. A wave that was clearly a resistance movement to a president and a Republican party that had made it clear they had little respect for women. She won her seat against all the odds in what had traditionally been a Republican seat.

At a fateful town hall meeting in Michigan, just days before the House was due to vote on impeaching Donald Trump, she stood in front of 400 vocal and partisan constituents to tell them why she was voting to impeach Trump.

She had bravely pre-announced her decision. By doing that she ensured a full house of people attending. She not only set the scene for a very loud and vocal reaction but could have attracted some of the more fringe people, those people who have shown they are not afraid of becoming violent and who support Trump no matter what.

Slotkin told the crowd that she had gone home for the weekend to go over all aspects of the evidence to ensure she was making her decision based on facts and not emotion. Ultimately she decided that Donald Trump had crossed a line by inviting a foreign government (Ukraine) to dig up dirt on his political rival, Joe Biden.

She could have done what many of her colleagues on both sides of the political spectrum were doing. She could have considered only her own political survival rather than considering the future of the country. She chose country. She told the people of Michigan what she was going to do and why. Some yelled and abused her while others stood and cheered.

Slotkin voted with her conscience; she stood in her 'truth' and was 100% prepared to accept the consequences of her decision.

> *'A leader is someone who has the clarity to know the right things to do, the confidence to know when she is wrong and the courage to do the right things even when it's hard.'*
>
> *Darcy Eikenber*

The intellectual warriors

Elizabeth Warren

Warren is a graduate of the University of Houston and Rutgers Law School. She taught law at several universities including Harvard before entering politics. Her specialty topic was bankruptcy law. She is a leading member of the American Democratic Party and considers herself a progressive.

Presumably because of her background in bankruptcy law, she

took a forceful position on reigning in banks after the 2007–08 financial crisis. She represented the Obama administration as the founder and first special adviser on the Consumer Financial Protection Bureau.

A passionate advocate for the environment, she urges her audiences and voters to take the scientific research on global warming seriously. She urges people to view the environmental situation we find ourselves in not as something to be terrified of or to bury our heads and deny, but as an opportunity to rebuild the American economy based on 100% clean energy, which is predicted will create millions of jobs in the process.

Warren was one of the frontrunners for the Democratic Party to take on Donald Trump in the 2020 presidential elections. Probably one of the most organised candidates on the trail, she is famous for her saying 'I have a plan for that' and she actually does have plans for most things affecting American families. Sadly she didn't get enough votes and was forced to withdraw her candidacy. However, I don't think that will be the last we hear of this gutsy woman.

Her passion and number one goal:

> *'We need to tackle the corruption in Washington that makes our government work for the wealthy and well-connected, but kicks dirt on everyone else, and put economic and political power back in the hands of the people.'*
>
> *Elizabeth Warren*

Malala Yousafzai

Malala acknowledges that being born a girl in Pakistan is not necessarily a great start in life. Fortunately for her, her father was a teacher and ran the girls' school in their village, so Malala was educated until the Taliban took over their town. Many things suddenly became forbidden: television, playing music and educating girls.

When she was just 11 years old, Malala spoke out against taking education away from girls, making her a prime target for the Taliban. Four years later, in October 2012, on her way home from school a gunman boarded her bus and shot her in the head. Malala was rushed to hospital and subsequently moved to a hospital in England where, despite dire predictions, she recovered.

This attempt on her life created an international outpouring of support and encouragement. The Taliban was denounced by governments, human rights organisations and feminist groups. Fifty leading Muslim clerics in Pakistan issued a fatwa against those who had tried to murder her. Undaunted, the Taliban announced that they had plans for a second attempt to remove her.

It was at this point that Malala realised she had two choices: she could hide away, play small and live a quiet life, or she could continue her outspoken calls to ensure that every girl has the opportunity to go to school.

Her advocacy and humanitarian work are now an international movement.

In 2011 she was nominated for the International Children's Peace Prize by Desmond Tutu. Although she didn't win the award, she was awarded the Nobel Peace Prize in 2014, becoming the youngest Nobel laureate in history.

In December 2012 UNESCO launched The Malala Fund for girls' education. Pakistan invested US$10 million immediately; Melinda and Bill Gates became patrons, as did Tim Cook, CEO of Apple, and Joe Gebbia, CPO of Airbnb. Starbucks and Avon cosmetics became sponsors.

'When the whole world is silent, even one voice becomes powerful. If people were silent nothing would change. We were scared, but our fear was not as strong as our courage. They thought that the bullets would silence us, but they failed.'

Malala

Angela Merkel

Angela Merkel's father was a theology student who accepted a pastorate in East Germany just weeks after she was born. She went on to study physics at Karl Marx University where she met her first husband, a fellow physics student, though the two eventually divorced.

Merkel worked as a member of the Central Institute of Physical Chemistry and was awarded a doctorate for her thesis on quantum chemistry. She became very involved in the German youth movement. Being an active member of the Free German Youth organisation led to a claim that she was involved in propaganda, a claim she vehemently denied. She was actually approached by the Ministry for State Security (Stasi) to become an informant. Merkel refused.

After the fall of the Berlin wall in 1989, Merkel joined the newly formed Democratic Awakening and very quickly became the party's press secretary. The shock to its members was when it was discovered that both their chairman, Wolfgang Schnur, and deputy chairman had been Stasi informants.

After this scandal, Merkel called upon the party to make a fresh start and is credited with being the person who virtually saved the party. On 10 April 2000, Merkel was elected head of the CDU, becoming the first woman and the first non-Catholic to lead the party, though she continued to face backlash from the party scandal.

On 22 November 2005, Merkel took office as Chancellor of

Germany, becoming the first woman, the first East German and, at age 51, the youngest person to hold the office.

Her second term was focused largely on her handling of the eurozone crisis. She implemented austerity measures so Europe could recover from the global financial crisis. Her greatest success was the implementation of a fiscal agreement that bound the signatories to operate within strict financial boundaries.

The European economy was still struggling as she entered her third term as chancellor. Massive discontent was looming in Greece, and Britain had voted to leave the EU altogether. Perhaps her greatest challenge in this third term was the Russian invasion of Crimea. She joined other Western leaders in accusing Russia of starting the conflict and spearheaded efforts to impose harsh sanctions against them.

She has also presided over the worst refugee crisis since the end of the Second World War, promising that she would keep Germany's borders open no matter the numbers. However, despite her best efforts, the sheer number of refugees forced her to temporarily suspend those open borders.

By now Merkel was entering her fourth term as chancellor, something no-one had ever done before. With obvious signs of health challenges, she declared that she would step down at the end of her term in 2021.

> *'The yearning for freedom cannot be contained by walls for long.'*
>
> *Angela Merkel*

The laugh-in-your-face warriors

Being a warrior can be exhausting work. It can seem such an endless journey with little light in the tunnel. No matter how passionate we are about changing something, it can seem like more steps backwards than forward. So when we meet 'cheeky' warriors, it lifts all of us who have a passion to make a difference.

Since Trump moved into the Oval Office and started his war on the world and in particular his war on anyone who dares to call him out, two people consistently and regularly make me laugh when they challenge him.

J.K. Rowling

Rowling worked as a bilingual researcher for Amnesty International when the idea for the Harry Potter story was born. Over the next seven years she lost her mother, gave birth to her first child, divorced her first husband and found herself in desperate financial straits. The first Harry Potter story was written in a café so she could keep warm and not run up her power bill.

She is the classic rags-to-riches story and would be one of the world's few female billionaires, except that she gives most of her money to charity. Even though she does this, she is still one of the wealthiest people in the world. I love her because she never misses an opportunity to rile Trump, and she does it so well.

Trump's tweet believing he is a great writer:

'After having written many best selling books and somewhat priding myself on my ability to write, it should be noted that the Fake News constantly likes to pour over my tweets looking for a mistake. I capitalize certain words only for emphasis not b/c they should be capitalized.'

Reply from @jk_rowling:

'pour'

hahahahahahahahahahahahahahahahahahahahahahahahahahahahaha
hahahahahahahahahahahahahahahahahahahahahahahahahahahahaha

hahahahahahahahahahahahaha *draws breath* hahahahahahahahahahahahahahahahahahahahahahahahahahahahaha hahahahahahahahahahahahahahahahahahahahahahahahahahahahaha hahahahahahahahahahaha

On the subject of his very large signature she tweeted a screenshot from the 'Study of Handwriting':

'An arrogant person, conceited, haughty, who needs to exhibit compliments and recognitions, tyrant tendencies, exhibitionist and phony personality that may become megalomaniac with lack of critical sense.'

On the subject of him having the nuclear codes:

'When a man this ignorant & easy to manipulate gets within sniffing distance of the nuclear codes, it's everyone's business.'

> *'Bigotry is probably the thing I detest the most.'*
>
> *J.K. Rowling*

Bette Midler

No-one could ever call Bette Midler a shrinking violet. I love this woman to bits. I cried an ocean when I watched her in *The Rose*; I still have to grab the tissue box when I hear her sing 'The Wind Beneath My Wings'. Bette is a redhead and a force to be reckoned with, so when Trump called her a 'washed up psycho', you just knew she would not take that lying down.

@realDonaldTrump:

'Washed up psycho @BetteMidler was forced to apologize for a statement she attributed to me that turned out to be totally fabricated by her in order to make 'your great president' look really bad. She got caught, just like the Fake News Media gets caught. A sick scammer!'

@BetteMidler responded:

'I want to thank everyone who came to my defense last night during my personal Battle of the Bulge with he who must not be named. Your wit and good nature really lifted my spirits; as a newly washed up psycho, I am very grateful for your thoughts and prayers.'

On Trump's excuse for the Access Hollywood comments:

'Donald Trump says it was just locker room talk, but does anyone really believe he has ever been in a gym?'

Midler went on to mock his sartorial style while in London and also to point out that:

'Trump said he was greeted by thousands in the UK, but they were actually thousands of protesters. How does he always hear the opposite of the truth? Donald, if you're reading this you SHOULD NOT slam your **** in a door!'

> *'My whole life has been spent waiting for an epiphany, a manifestation of God's presence, the kind of transcendent, magical experience that lets you see your place in the big picture. And that is what I had with my first compost heap.'*
>
> *Bette Midler*

The rambunctious, LOUD and unapologetic warriors

Emma González

Who was not horrified by the Parkland shooting? Yet another senseless massacre of kids just wanting an education. And who was not impressed with the kids that stepped forward and became the voice of the anti-gun movement?

One of the female leaders of Parkland activism was Emma González; her mother is a maths tutor and her father a cyber security attorney. The family emigrated from Cuba to America in 1968.

On the day of the school shooting she was in the auditorium with dozens of other students. When shots were heard they tried to escape but were told to stay where they were and to take cover. They were kept in the auditorium for two hours while the shootings took place.

Imagine the terror.

Within days of the killing of 17 students, González turned her horror into activism. She has delivered numerous speeches since that fateful day, including at a gun control rally when she called BS on Trump and the NRA for continually refusing to tighten gun laws.

Along with other Parkland survivors she launched 'March for Our Lives', a not-for-profit, non-partisan organisation calling for tougher gun laws and encouraging young voters to register to vote in the 2020 presidential election.

Variety magazine invited her to be one of their five 2018 Power of Women honourees, which she was reluctant to accept, not wanting to draw attention exclusively to herself. Thankfully, she saw the bigger picture and accepted the award.

Her mother was interviewed by *60 Minutes* and said that she was a normal kid until the shooting.

> *'It's like she built herself a pair of wings out of balsa wood and duct tape and jumped off a building and we're just, like, running along beneath her with a net, which she doesn't want or think that she needs.'*
>
> *Beth González, mother of Emma González*

Alexandria Ocasio-Cortez

The youngest woman ever elected to Congress, Ocasio-Cortez beat a 10-term Democratic incumbent who at that stage was the fourth-ranking Democrat.

After just one year in office she has convinced every presidential candidate to support her Green New Deal. She has raised more money than any other Democrat, even overtaking the money raised by Nancy Pelosi.

She is fearless in challenging the status quo. She grills people at hearings, asking questions that really should have been asked by much more experienced senators who seem quite happy to use their precious time in the spotlight to pontificate and grandstand. Not so for Alexandria.

She has also challenged the expectations of how young women (particularly young women of colour) should behave. She absolutely takes on those older white men in politics who think women should be seen and not heard.

She refuses to take donations from rich donors; she spends her time studying policy and preparing to ask those stultifying questions. She called out the appalling rationale for separating children from their parents and the inhuman conditions families were being kept in on the border.

She famously grilled Mark Zuckerberg over his willingness to let political parties post political adverts that were clearly lies.

She is polarising the right wing of politics; apparently Fox News can't get enough of her. Trump has labelled her a 'communist' and the GOP use her as the example of the dangers of socialism, and she simply doesn't care what these people think of her. She is 100% her own person.

Unlike most politicians who want to have their cushy job for life, she has said quite categorically that she doesn't care if she is a one-term member of Congress. She believes that 'you can make ten years' worth of change in one term if you're not afraid'.

> *'People often say, how are you gonna pay for it? And I find the question so puzzling because, how do you pay for something that's more affordable? How do you pay for cheaper rent? How do you pay for anything, you just pay for it.'*
>
> *Alexandria Ocasio-Cortez*

The never-give-up warriors

Jane Fonda

Despite being part of the amazing Fonda family and despite having massive success as an actress in her own right, Jane Fonda famously risked her career by taking physical and vocal exception to America's involvement in the Vietnam War. America took exception to her exception and dubbed her 'Hanoi Jane'. She was blacklisted in Hollywood and her movie career was virtually over.

Undaunted, she took this time out and joined forces with Robin Morgan and Gloria Steinem to co-found the Women's Media Center, an organisation dedicated to helping women find their voice in whatever profession they choose.

She protested the war in Iraq and is a passionate advocate for ending violence against women. Happily describing herself as a feminist, Fonda is now equally involved in the climate change marches. On the eve of her 82nd birthday, she set out to bring 82 people along to a march so they could be arrested together; 138 people answered her call and marched alongside her including her friend Gloria Steinem and actresses Sally Field and Lily Tomlin.

Not content with simply marching and getting arrested, she

decided to use her fame and celebrity to raise awareness and create a sense of urgency. And so 'Fire Drill Friday' was launched. Everyone who shows up dresses in red and they are trained in being 'arrested'. The protests are to support the Green New Deal but also to raise awareness as to how climate change affects all manner of things: access to fresh drinking water, loss of air quality, loss of habitat, loss of homes.

On 3 January 2020, Sam Waterston, co-star of *Grace and Frankie,* joined her and was arrested for a second time. Iain Armitage, 'Young Sheldon', spoke after one of the marches and wished Greta Thunberg a happy birthday as she turned 17 that very day.

Fonda credits Greta with her getting involved in protests again. The decision to wear red (Fonda admitted she normally never wore red) was to be visible. She bought a red coat on sale and promises it will be the last thing she buys as she raises awareness of consumerism and the effect that is having on the planet. When Lily Tomlin joined her and got arrested, she declared: 'We have got to stop hugging and start saving the trees; these corporations are making oodles of money on the front end, oodles of money on the back end.'

Fonda proudly and fearlessly acknowledges she is a feminist and a revolutionary. She says: 'To be a revolutionary, you have to be a human being. You have to care about people who have no power. We cannot always control our thoughts, but we can control our words, and repetition impresses the subconscious, and we are then masters of the situation. If the career you have chosen has some unexpected inconvenience, console yourself by reflecting that no career is without them.'

> *'The young climate strikers have been very, very instrumental in making this shift to where we're talking about fossil fuels. We should be very grateful to the young people and the students who are sacrificing so much to call our attention to it. You know, you can't solve a problem if you're not naming it. And so today we*

want to name it in a big way. Because to slow down and stop the climate crisis, we must stop burning fossil fuels.'

Jane Fonda

Lucy Lawless

With a name like Lawless (she married a Garth Lawless and not only took his name but kept that name during her movie career), how could you not be a warrior?

Lucy is a New Zealand actress and donned her famous leather outfit to play the part of Xena, warrior princess. Now back in New Zealand she is a wife and mother, yet when, on 27 February 2012, an opportunity came to challenge oil drilling in the seas of New Zealand, she metaphorically donned her Xena warrior outfit and chained herself to the mast of an oil-drilling ship.

Lawless and five other Greenpeace protesters were arrested after spending four days on board the *Noble Discoverer,* which was due to travel to the Arctic to drill for oil. The activists climbed the 53-metre drilling derrick and unfurled their banners. By doing this and by refusing to move, they prevented the ship from leaving Port Taranaki and created international awareness to their cause.

Lawless admits to being absolutely terrified during the protest but she did it anyway. The activists were arrested and sentenced to community work. Shell Oil and Todd Energy, who had contracted the ship, originally demanded NZ$600,000 in reparation. Judge Allan Roberts, who heard the arguments, sentenced each of the activists to 120 hours of community work and ordered them to each pay NZ$651.44 in reparation to the port.

Lawless was delighted with the outcome, saying that her sentence was 'a total victory' and that 'Shell got basically booted out of court because they were ludicrous from the start.' Asked where she would do her community service, Lawless joked: 'In a public toilet near you.'

Undaunted and undeterred, on 21 July 2017, she joined Greenpeace activists who took to the icy waters in inflatable boats to challenge the Statoil Songa Enabler oil rig 275 kilometres off the Norwegian coast. Despite all research to the contrary, Statoil and Norway joined forces to aggressively search for oil in the waters of the Barents Sea.

Activist Joanna Sustento from the Philippines was with Lawless and 19 other nationalities who took part in the protest. Sustento lost almost all her family to super-typhoon Haiyan in 2013 and now classes herself as a climate change survivor.

Sustento said: 'It is hard for me to grasp and accept that a government like Norway's is opening up new Arctic oil drilling, knowing full well it will put families and homes in other parts of the world at risk. I'm here in the Arctic to see this irresponsibility with my own eyes; share my story about the human consequences of climate change and call on the Norwegian government to put a stop to this dangerous search for new oil.'

In a recent interview Lawless admits that she is 'brutally disappointed' in her generation for not stepping up and doing enough about climate change.

> *'How dare we as parents abrogate our responsibility to protect our children? If anything brings out the warrior in me, it is that. It's about honouring all life on the planet; we all rise together.'*
>
> *Lucy Lawless*

The spiritual warriors

Louise Hay

My doctor called at 8 p.m. one night (never the harbinger of good news) to say I needed to come to his surgery the next day. The results of a blood test had returned and he wasn't happy with the diagnosis. I told him I wouldn't sleep a wink if he didn't tell me what his concerns were. I have a history of breast cancer in my family and this was my greatest fear. He advised me that some 'abnormal cells' had shown up in my tests. After more visits and further tests I was found to be clear, but his next words literally floored me. He said: 'So when are you going to get your life sorted out, Ann?'

My long-term marriage had broken up suddenly the year before and I thought I was coping with that shock really well. I'd managed to find a job, which, after 10 years of being out of the workforce, was a minor miracle. I was putting food on the table and paying the mortgage so we had a roof over our heads. My teen kids appeared to be coping with all the changes, so I didn't quite understand what he was saying.

He recommended I read Louise Hay's book *You Can Heal Your Life*. So I did. And I was truly blown away. I got the message, his and hers. I put the book on my shelf and got on with working to keep my kids fed and the mortgage paid.

Came the day several years later when I was sort of diagnosed with chronic fatigue syndrome. I say 'sort of' because in those days no-one quite knew what chronic fatigue was. A few years later, this condition became better known as ME (myalgic encephalomyelitis). The problem for sufferers is that it has no visible signs of illness other than the fact that the patient has zero energy. Basically I could hardly get out of bed; the simplest tasks exhausted me, even having a shower required the rest of the day in bed to sleep off the energy I had used to just wash my hair.

As women, when we complain about any health issues, we are familiar with being told 'it's all in your mind' and according to Louise Hay, mostly, our dis-ease actually *is* in our minds.

Once I started investigating my condition I realised I was dealing with the disease of ME, Me, me.

I had experienced those magical first six years of my life being brought up by my beautiful grandparents, then my mother married and I was removed from my warm, loving, happy home to one that was none of those things. I experienced neglect and sexual abuse for years. At 13 years old I realised I had to escape. For the first time I got serious about my education. I knew getting some good grades at school would be my passport out of there. As a result of those grades, I was able to qualify for that one year secretarial course and I got the heck out of there.

The problem with years of abuse is that it settles into the core of your being. We may think we've dealt with it, but mostly we've just put a sticking plaster over the wounds. That's what my doctor recognised even though I thought I'd covered things up really well.

Of course I was going to be 'damaged'. My self-esteem was in the pits; my self-worth was none existent; I was basically surviving on determination and the need to put that one foot in front of the other.

Chronic fatigue, or ME, showed up once my kids were off and independent. It was almost as if my body said, 'Okay, I've kept you going all these years, but now I need some attention. You need to look after *me*.'

And so began several years of counselling to deal with those dark years; to get the poison out of my system; to get on with the rest of my life free from the 'baggage' I'd been subconsciously carrying around as a result of those early years.

Hay's book is now my first port of call when I get any condition — skin complaints, headaches, coughs, colds, sores, throat infections, whatever. I check with Louise, hate what she tells me and then set about healing myself.

Can I heal everything? Of course not. I broke my leg on a hike once; I couldn't heal that, but I did speed up the healing process by using her suggested affirmations. However, and in particular, if I get a sore throat or heartburn or sinus, I check what Louise says about that:

Throat: The ability to speak up for oneself. Swallowed anger. Stifled creativity.

Affirmation: I express myself freely and joyously. I speak up for myself with ease.

Heartburn: Fear, fear, fear. Clutching fear.

Affirmation: I breathe freely and fully. I am safe. I trust the process of life.

Sinus: Irritation to a person; who is getting up your nose?

Affirmation: I declare peace and harmony dwell in me and surround me. All is well in my world.

> *'You've been criticizing yourself for years and it hasn't worked. Try approving of yourself and see what happens.'*
>
> *Louise Hay*

Oprah Winfrey

I doubt that there is a woman in the world who hasn't been influenced by Oprah. She started her career as a TV anchor at the age of 19 after graduating from Tennessee State University. She quickly realised that news reporting was too constraining for her natural talents and moved into co-hosting a Baltimore morning show, *People Are Talking*.

Oprah had found her groove: talking to and interviewing people was then and always will be her greatest talent.

Her next move was to Chicago. She was employed in the hope that she could energise a faltering talk show, *AM Chicago*. She did more than energise the show: it became so popular that it was renamed *The Oprah Winfrey Show*.

Oprah is also an amazing actress. If you've ever seen *The Color Purple*, you will have loved her portrayal of Sofia, a young African-American slave subjected to all manner of abuse but who found hope and self-worth through two strong female companions.

She then formed her own production company, Harpo Productions, where she began buying the rights to many literary works. She bought the rights to *Before Women Had Wings*, a movie she produced and starred in. She did the same with the rights to *Beloved*, where she also had a starring role. She finds and promotes movies that may never have seen the light of day without her. She produced and appeared in *Selma*, a movie about Martin Luther King, which was nominated for Best Picture and won Best Original Song at the Academy Awards.

Who can forget her book club? She would announce the chosen book a couple of weeks before her show and the book would be a guaranteed bestseller. This had a flow-on effect to the publishing sector and book sales — an industry that had been flagging since the advent of e-books and e-readers.

Not content with movies and books and interviews, Oprah launched *O, The Oprah Magazine* and *O At Home* alongside any number of philanthropic initiatives. Her Angel Network funded a US$40 million school for disadvantaged girls in South Africa.

Her awards are numerous: she was a Kennedy Center honouree in 2010; she received the Jean Hersholt Humanitarian Award from the Academy of Motion Picture Arts and Sciences; and in 2013 she was awarded the Presidential Medal of Freedom, the highest civilian award, which recognises 'an especially meritorious contribution to the security or national interests of the United States, world peace, cultural or other significant public or private endeavors'.

I would go so far as to say that no woman in modern history has had such an influence on women, minorities and the human condition than she has.

> *'Everybody has a calling. And your real job in life is to figure out as soon as possible what that is, who you were meant to be, and to begin to honor that in the best way possible for yourself.'*
>
> *Oprah Winfrey*

The bravest of brave warriors

Marie Yovanovitch

Yovanovitch was, up until recently, the American Ambassador to Ukraine. Born in Canada after her parents fled the Soviet Union, she is a fluent Russian speaker and had previously served in a variety of posts. She was Deputy Director of the Russian Desk in the US Department of State; Ambassador to Kyrgyzstan; Ambassador to Armenia; Principal Deputy Assistant Secretary for the Bureau of European and Eurasian Affairs.

In every post she distinguished herself.

While Ambassador to Ukraine she found herself on the wrong side of three men: Rudy Giuliani, Trump's personal lawyer; Gordon Sondland, United States Ambassador to the European Union; and Donald Trump himself.

They claimed she was impeding their investigations into corruption in Ukraine, when in fact the opposite would appear to be true. She was impeding *them* in launching a fake investigation into Joe Biden, Trump's key political rival, and Biden's son

Hunter. Hunter Biden had been on the board of Burisma, a Ukrainian gas company.

Investigations have been conducted into Hunter Biden working for Burisma and though ethical watchdogs have criticised his decision to work for this company at the time his father was Vice President to President Obama, no evidence of any wrongdoing or illegal activity on his part or his father's have been uncovered. Hunter Biden denies ever discussing his role with his father other than one brief conversation where his father had said, 'I hope you know what you're doing.'

In May 2019, Yovanovitch was relieved of her position.

Donald Trump had spotted an opportunity to get 'dirt' on his main opponent, Joe Biden, via his son. With the removal of Yovanovitch, he had cleared the way to do just that. On the infamous July 2019 phone call with newly elected President Zelensky when talk turned to financial aid, the US$400 million that Ukraine desperately needed to fight the Russian invasion, money that had been signed off by Congress, Trump said, 'I'd like you to do me a favour though?' In other words, in exchange for that money I need you to set up an investigation into Burisma, Joe Biden and his son Hunter Biden.

The money was frozen by the White House for several weeks while Trump involved Rudy Giuliani and the attorney general Bill Barr in coercing President Zelensky to accommodate a totally tenuous investigation into the Bidens. Trump was adamant that he wanted the newly elected president of Ukraine to start an investigation into their activities, which would allow him to besmirch his political rival in advance of the 2020 presidential elections.

Fortunately, when the July call was made, as is the White House practice when POTUS speaks to a foreign leader, many people were actually on the call listening and taking notes. One of the people on that call laid a complaint, becoming the famous 'whistle-blower', and set off the impeachment process.

Suddenly the aid was released.

The Democratic Party, via the House Intelligence Committee, launched an investigation into what they saw as an abuse of power and began interviewing the various people who had knowledge of what had happened in Ukraine. Marie Yovanovitch was one of the star witnesses. Despite knowing that she had been under surveillance by the very people who were supposed to protect ambassadors abroad, she appeared and gave testimony to the House Intelligence Committee, stating that in the middle of the night she had received a phone call by a State Department official to return home 'on the next plane' because of concerns 'up the street', a phrase she knew to mean the White House.

Even as she was giving her testimony, Trump was tweeting about her, criticising her track record. When Adam Schiff suggested this was witness intimidation and that 'some of us here take witness intimidation very, very seriously', Trump's response was 'I'm allowed to speak up'. This spiteful and childish reaction from the President of the United States!

Her courage literally under fire even while testifying drew praise from Republican representative Will Hurd, who said: 'You're tough as nails and you're smart as hell. You're a great example of what our ambassadors should be like. You're an honor to your family, you are an honor to the foreign service, you are an honor to this country, and I thank you for all that you have done and will continue to do on behalf of your country.' Yovanovitch asked these questions in her opening statement:

> *'How could our system fail like this? How is it that foreign corrupt interests could manipulate our government?'*
>
> *Marie Yovanovitch*

Fiona Hill

Fiona Hill was born in the UK and is the daughter of a coal miner. After the closure of most of the UK mines, her family struggled to make ends meet. Fiona and her sister worked at all and any odd jobs, from washing cars to waitressing to help out with the family income.

Hill studied history and Russian at the University of St Andrews in Scotland and was an exchange student in the Soviet Union. She was encouraged to apply for a graduate programme in the US by an American professor. She studied at Harvard and gained her master's degree in Russian and went on to gain a PhD in history.

Her professional career began in the research department at the John F Kennedy School of Government and from there she became a national analyst of Russia and Eurasia. She is a member of the Council of Foreign Relations and by 1999 was director of Harvard University's Strengthening Democratic Institutions project.

She was an intelligence analyst under George W Bush and Barack Obama and was appointed by Donald Trump in 2017 as Deputy Assistant to the President and Senior Director for European and Russian Affairs on the Trump National Security Council staff. She resigned this position in July 2019.

As with Marie Yovanovitch, Hill was called to testify in a closed-door deposition where she was questioned for 10 hours by members of the US Congress as part of the impeachment hearing against Donald Trump.

She was invited to testify again at the public hearing in November 2019, where she raised her concerns about the involvement of Ambassador Gordon Sondland in what was happening in Ukraine. Sondland was not a career diplomat; he was a businessman who had made a large donation to the Trump campaign and was handsomely rewarded for those contributions with an ambassadorship. Hill testified that she was concerned when she read various emails from Sondland. She was particularly concerned with the recipients of these emails, people she felt didn't have the security clearances to be involved in such communications. She further believed that Sondland was discussing matters that she believed were outside his remit.

She testified that she felt 'he was being involved in a domestic political errand, and we were being involved in national security foreign policy. And those two things had just diverged. That divergence between the domestic political errand and official policy cuts to the heart of the scandal.' She went on to say that 'The Russians' interests are frankly to delegitimize our entire presidency. The goal of the Russians [in 2016] was really to put *whoever* became the president — by trying to tip their hands on one side of the scale — under a cloud.'

Tim Miller, a writer for *The Bulwark,* described her as the 'Impeachment Queen', saying 'she's not the hero we deserve, she's the hero we need'. He went on to further praise her performance under such enormous pressure, saying: 'Queen Fiona, who saved us from this impeachment death march. In control. Unphased [sic] by the partisan nonsense. Clear-eyed about Vladimir Putin. Not jaded or beaten down by the avalanche of acrimony and foolishness that she has been dealt in the past two years. A woman who wants only to serve the adopted country she loves.'

> *'... some of you on this committee appear to believe that Russia and its security services did not conduct a campaign against our country — and that perhaps, somehow, for some reason, Ukraine did. This is a fictional narrative that has been perpetrated and propagated by the Russian security services themselves. ... The unfortunate truth is that Russia was the foreign power that systematically attacked our democratic institutions in 2016.'*
>
> *Fiona Hill*

The magnificent 'don't-mess-with-me' warriors

Kamala Harris

Harris is actually the daughter of a warrior and the granddaughter of a warrior.

An American lawyer and member of the Democratic Party, Harris entered the race to become POTUS in 2019 but withdrew in December that same year. Born in Oakland, California, Harris is a graduate of Howard University and the University of California, Hastings College of Law.

In 1990, long before her aspirations to become president emerged, she was a deputy district attorney in Alameda County, California, where she specialised in child sexual abuse trials, which she acknowledged was a particularly difficult and heart-breaking kind of prosecution given that juries are more likely to believe the word of an adult over the word of a child.

She went on to become the 27th district attorney of San Francisco from 2004 to 2011, the first Jamaican American and the first Indian American attorney general in California to do so. She progressed to becoming the 32nd attorney general for the same district from 2011 to 2017.

As a senator she is a passionate advocate for single-payer healthcare, for creating a pathway to citizenship for undocumented immigrants, and for banning assault rifles. She also campaigns on lowering the tax burden on lower-income families while raising taxes for corporations and the wealthiest people in America.

Her mother, Shyamala, is breast-cancer scientist who immigrated to America in 1960 to pursue a doctorate in endocrinology. Shyamala is a Tamil Indian, an upper-class Brahman whose bloodline can be traced back over 1000 years.

Even before Shyamala came to America she was described as a feminist. Her concern was that the women who did her family's laundry were often the victims of domestic violence.

Harris's father is a Stanford University economics professor who emigrated from Jamaica in 1961 to study economics at UC Berkeley. Harris identifies as both African American and Indian American and is a descendant from a Jamaican slave owner.

Harris knows that female candidates have a hard time when applying for political positions, but suggests that black females have an even tougher battle. She is aware that most 'whites' see black women as servants, maids or cooks. Her recommendations to younger women of colour who have aspirations to be more than maids or cooks is to become active on social, cultural and charitable boards. It gives women a starting point, a place to learn the ropes; a way to build networks and to start to earn respect.

It was during various congressional hearings that Kamala made her real mark. She fearlessly questioned Jeff Sessions, Brett Kavanaugh and Bill Barr, the newly appointed attorney general.

Her questioning of Jeff Sessions as to whether he had communicated with any Russians during the 2016 presidential campaign was met with endless replies of 'I don't remember' or 'I don't recall'. She had him virtually begging for mercy when he said that her questioning 'made him nervous'.

Similarly her questioning of Brett Kavanaugh as he was being vetted for a lifetime appointment on the Supreme Court left him floundering. Given that Kavanaugh is a staunch anti-abortionist no matter a woman's or a girl's situation, she asked him if he knew of any laws 'that the government has to make over the male body'. After a very long silence, he replied, 'I'm not aware of any right now, Senator.'

And finally her eviscerating of Bill Barr when she asked, 'Has the President or anyone at the White House ever asked or suggested that you open an investigation of anyone? Yes or no, please, sir.' A question that caused him to huff and puff while trying his very best not to answer the question and possibly perjure himself. By his actions he let America know that he probably had.

What was stunning about these three situations is that all three men are seasoned politicians, yet here they were, all three of them, unable to answer questions they must have known they would be asked.

Matt Stieb, writing for the New York *Intelligencer*, says: 'Though Kamal Harris's record as a prosecutor might not be helping her run for the Democratic presidential nomination, her past role as California's top cop has certainly prepared her for her role on the Senate Judiciary Committee. During Attorney General William Barr's testimony regarding his handling of the Mueller report, Harris cemented her reputation, already established during the Kavanaugh hearings, as the Senate Democrats' most acute questioner.'

She was soundly berated by many male Republican senators for what they saw as aggressive questioning; these were the self-same senators who had grilled Christine Blasey Ford, who is *not* a seasoned politician. Yet no-one complained about their behaviours or the way she was treated. It seems if men aggressively question a witness that is seen as them being assertive; if a woman does the same she is viewed as a ball-breaker. Funny standards.

She may never be POTUS, but imagine if one day, when a Democrat sits in the Oval Office, she replaces Bill Barr as the attorney general. I'd suggest Sessions, Kavanaugh and Barr will be heading for the hills or purchasing land on a remote island somewhere with no connectivity.

> *'I grew up hearing stories about my grandmother — my mother's mother — who used to go to villages in India in her little VW bug.*

My grandmother would take a bullhorn and make sure women in those villages knew how to access birth control.'

Kamala Harris

Nancy Pelosi

Nancy is the 52nd Speaker of the House of Representatives. She made history in 2007 when she was the first ever elected female in the role. She made history once again when she returned as the Speaker in January 2019. Being the Speaker makes her second in line to the President.

She is a passionate advocate for lower health costs, increased worker pay and cleaning up the environment. She similarly wants to clean up the corruption prevalent in Washington.

In 2009, she pushed through the landmark American Clean Energy and Security Act, a bill designed to create clean energy jobs, combat the climate crisis, and move America towards a clean economy. The legislation was blocked by Republicans in the United States Senate (shame on them), which sent a strong signal to the world about the United States' commitment or lack thereof to be part of the fight against global warming.

She has represented San Francisco as their senator for 31 years, has led the house Democrats for 16 years, and in 2013 she was inducted into the National Women's Hall of Fame in Seneca Falls, the birthplace of the American women's rights movement.

Pelosi is a tireless worker. She was congratulated on heading up one of the 'most productive Congresses in history' by Congressional scholar Norman Ornstein. President Obama acknowledged her as being an 'extraordinary leader for the American people' and the *Christian Science Monitor* declared 'make no mistake, Nancy Pelosi is the most powerful woman in American politics and the most powerful House Speaker since Sam Rayburn'.

She was instrumental with Obama in launching the American Recovery and Reinvestment Act in 2009, which aimed to create and save millions of jobs and to provide relief for families. Perhaps her most prominent initiative was the design of the Affordable Care Act guaranteeing health cover for all Americans.

She is determined to rein in the big banks; she is no friend to Wall Street. She is determined to expand educational opportunities for lower-income families and in 2010 she led Congress in passing child nutrition and food safety legislation.

She refuses to give up the fight for accountability and transparency in government. Under her leadership the toughest ethics reforms were implemented while an independent ethics panel was instigated. She is similarly determined to fight the corporate takeover of US elections.

She has proven to be the toughest of negotiators.

Despite the Republican Party seemingly intent on taking away all and every assistance given to families while gifting the most generous tax breaks to corporates and billionaires, it seems she will not be beaten down. Even post Trump's election, she negotiated a five-year extension of soon-to-expire wind and solar tax credits and won a US$3.2 billion increase in opioid funding, a US$3 billion increase for medical and the largest funding increase for Child Care and Development Block Grants.

The Nancy Pelosi handclap: on 5 February 2019 Donald Trump gave his State of the Union address while Nancy sat directly behind him — at times she rolled her eyes at his comments, other times she ignored him and read something on her knee, but on conclusion of his speech, she did what has been described as 'the walrus handclap', an incredibly patronising/sarcastic 'Well done, Donald.' NOT!

Her second moment was when a journalist asked her if she hated Trump just hours after she announced articles of impeachment against him. Her instant reply was 'I don't hate anybody and as a Catholic I resent your using the hate word in a sentence that addresses me.' She went on to say that she was bringing the articles against him to protect the American Constitution as a result of what she saw was a president consistently violating his oath of office.

Her third moment of defiance was after Trump's State of the Union speech on 5 February 2020. A speech which, as usual, was full of lies and innuendo; a solemn occasion he turned into a reality TV show, even awarding the highest military honour in America, the Medal of Honor, to a known misogynist, white supremacist and conspiracy theorist.

Behind Trump's back Nancy stood literally tearing his speech into pieces. When asked afterwards why she did that, her response was that it was because she could not find a page that did not have a lie on it.

> *'What the Republicans have said is, rather than touch one hair on the head of the wealthiest people, people who make over US$1 million a year, they're saying "Seniors should pay $6000 more a year, but please don't let us ask the wealthiest to do their fair share".'*
>
> *Nancy Pelosi*

The warrior to beat all warriors

Greta Thunberg

Who can ever forget the picture of a little girl sitting outside the Swedish parliament with her one and only banner? Who would have believed that this one little girl could have mobilised a global movement of people who stand with her? Who would have believed that the opposition to her would be so vitriolic and vehement?

Despite suggestions to the contrary, her parents were actually not in favour of her setting out to be the face of climate change. Greta was diagnosed with Asperger's at the age of 12, something she describes as her superpower.

According to her father she had struggled with depression for three or four years before she started her activism. He went on to say that 'she stopped talking, stopped going to school and finally, she stopped eating'. Her mother, an opera singer, cancelled all engagements and both parents decided to spend more time with both their daughters given what Greta was going through.

But Greta is rising above it all.

Once again, according to her father, despite the hate that comes her way, her activism has helped her become a very happy person: 'She dances around, laughs a lot and is in a very good place.'

Sir David Attenborough lauds Greta with bringing climate change to the masses, something he has been trying to do for over 20 years. She was nominated for the 2019 Nobel Peace Prize and, like Malala before her, didn't win, but she went on to become *Time* magazine's Person of the Year.

The article in *Time* magazine regarding her selection stresses that 'the world's temperature rise since the Industrial Revolution will hit the 1.5°C mark—an eventuality that scientists warn will expose some 350 million additional people to drought and push roughly 120 million people into extreme poverty by 2030'. The article went on to say: 'For decades, researchers and activists have struggled to get world leaders to take the climate threat seriously. But this year, an unlikely teenager somehow got the world's attention.'

When she famously said, 'I don't want your hope, I don't want you to be hopeful. I want you to panic and act as if your house was on fire', she spoke for billions of us who fear time really is running out. Yet climate deniers keep denying and berate Greta at every opportunity calling her hysterical, angry, over-emotional and even 'too loud for people to handle' and she is regularly told to 'get back to school'.

Older white men in particular seem to be the ones most threatened by her. Andrew Bolt, a *Herald Sun* columnist, has labelled her as 'freakishly influential' and having 'many mental disorders'; *Sky News* commentator Chris Kenny suggested that she is a 'hysterical teenager who needs to be cared for'.

Jennifer O'Connell, a writer for the *Irish Times*, suggests that 'Part of the reason she [Thunberg] inspires such rage, of course, is blindingly obvious. Climate change is terrifying. The Amazon is burning. So too is the Savannah. Parts of the Arctic are on fire. Sea levels are rising. There are more vicious storms and wildfires and droughts and floods. Denial is easier than confronting the terrifying truth.'

I've noticed myself that if I post any messages about climate change or environmental issues on social media, women absolutely seem to share my concerns, while older white men basically rage at me telling me what a load of tosh all this climate change stuff is. It's almost as if any mention of climate change attacks their very manhood, when in fact Greta is only vocalising what millions of people are witnessing with their own eyes and in their own lives.

In my humble opinion, Greta is doing what she is here to do, and I personally support her every step of the way.

> *'The eyes of all future generations are upon you. And if you choose to fail us, I say we will never forgive you.'*
>
> *Greta Thunberg, UN Climate Action Summit, New York, 2019*

Questions regarding Chapter 2

There were 25 warriors in this chapter.

Who impressed you?

Who terrified you?

Who repelled you?

Who had you never heard of?

Who will you now follow?

Which 'warrior' are you most like?

Which 'warrior' are you least like?

Has there been a time in your life when you became a warrior?

How did that go?

Have there been times in your life when you *wish* you'd been more warrior-like?

If a situation like that ever occurs again, will you now have the courage to stand your ground?

3

HOW MEN SET THE TABLE

'The women's suffrage movement is only the small edge of the wedge, if we allow women to vote it will mean the loss of social structure and the rise of every liberal cause under the sun. Women are well represented by their fathers, brothers and husbands.'

Sir Winston Churchill

Understanding paternalism

The word paternalism is from the Latin *pater* meaning 'father', and *paternus* meaning 'fatherly'. It wasn't until the late 19th century that the term 'paternalism' appeared in our language.

I never knew my father. My grandfather was my male role model. He was an absolute angel. He taught me every plant, every tree, every bird, he even taught me how to knit! He was the kind version of paternalism. He wanted nothing but the best for me, was always there for me and I don't think I ever heard him raise his voice. Exactly what any child would want from a parent — male or female.

If we go back in time several millennia to the days where humans lived in caves, men hunted for food, women looked after children and cooked the food. Even after leaving cave dwelling for more civilised dwellings, men were still the breadwinners; women traditionally stayed home with their parents until they married, then, once married, their life became one of having babies, looking after children and being the home-maker.

It wasn't unusual for women to have a baby every year until they either died of exhaustion or simply stopped being able to have children. It wasn't unusual for families to have anything from six to 15 children in Victorian times; partly due to lack of reliable and safe birth control but also because prior to the introduction of a social welfare system, children were an economic asset to poorer families. Once they were of working age and could bring home a wage, children had to contribute to the family coffers. In those poor families, children would be sent out to work as soon as they were able to run an errand or use a broom.

Industrialisation created a massive gap for workers. Factory owners didn't much care what age people were as long as they could do a job. It wasn't unusual for children as young as eight to work in factories and mines. Chimney sweeps were usually small boys who could climb up the inside of a chimney, cleaning the soot as they went! In factories they were useful at fetching and carrying between spinning or weaving machines; in coal mines children were especially valued because they could crawl into much smaller areas to reach small veins of coal, spaces grown men couldn't reach.

Imagine the terror of that for a child.

Caring Victorians were horrified at this exploitation of children, and the Factory Act (1833) prohibited children younger than nine to be employed. It also limited the number of hours children between nine and 13 could work. The Mines Act (1842) raised the starting age of colliery workers to 10 years.

Britain ended the exploitation of children, yet today we still see countries doing to their children what was found to be repugnant in the mid 1800s.

How paternalism and child labour are linked

In Somalia 76% of children five to 14 are child labourers. They are employed in the fishing sector, agriculture, construction and mining. They are also seen begging and hawking. All of this is horrific enough, but they are also trained as soldiers and are engaged in real conflicts. Child trafficking is not uncommon.

In Pakistan some 13% of children aged 10 to 14 are child labourers, the vast majority working in fishing and agriculture but also on tea stalls and, sadly, in garbage scavenging. The glass jewellery industry, carpet weaving, coal mining, the brick kiln sector and even the auto industry employ children.

India has an estimated 33 million child labourers. Despite India's economy growing rapidly, the wealth hasn't flowed down to the poorest families. The use of child labour, far from decreasing, has actually increased over recent years.

In Nigeria it is estimated that over 15 million children below the age of 14 work in similar industries to those in Pakistan and India. Girls enter the workforce earlier than boys, mostly in domestic work.

And, of course, when children are working they are not being educated. So countries perpetuate the problem — large families tend to be poor families and just as the early Victorian families discovered, children become a source of revenue and the practice perpetuates the cycle of poor education and poverty.

Shame on the following corporates, which still use child labour.

Nestlé: Terry Collingsworth, a human rights lawyer, filed a lawsuit in October 2018 taking the organisation to task for its continued use of child labour. Another human rights activist, Danell Tomasella, has taken a separate class action suit against them — she believes they are lying to consumers by failing to disclose continued use of child labour. Their excuse is that their profits would be affected and how else could they return shareholder investment?!

H&M have faced allegations of neglect to worker rights throughout their various factories. Reports suggest that they continue to use child labour in factories in Myanmar, Bangladesh and Cambodia, paying as little as 13 pence per hour. Despite a massive drop in profits in 2018 because of the use of child labour, they keep going with the practice using as their excuse that the legal working age in Myanmar is 14.

Philip Morris. In 2010 the company actually admitted that children as young as 10 had been forced into working on their tobacco farms in Kazakhstan. As if that wasn't shameful enough, they have a practice of taking passports off families so they can't escape the farms. Even in 2018 a *Guardian* investigation discovered that children working on their farms in Malawi 'is rampant'.

Microsoft. Triple shame on this company because despite their reputation as being a top employer and the Gates Foundation being so philanthropic, it was discovered that in 2018 children as young as seven were being used in the Democratic Republic of Congo to extract cobalt for up to 12 hours per day. Cobalt is toxic! Once found out, they moved quickly to address the issue, but Amnesty International remains sceptical, stating that there is still a long way to go before they fully redeem themselves.

Apple has a reputation of being one of the most innovative brands on the planet, but they too have been found to use schoolchildren to make their iPhone X.

New Look is also involved in child labour practices in Myanmar. They apparently have at least agreed this is unacceptable and to work with suppliers and partners to address the use of children. They have implemented a remediation programme where underage children are removed from factories and returned to school. They still have to address the issue of the raw cotton they use for their clothing, which is sourced in Uzbekistan and uses child labour — their rationale is that sourcing the cotton is their contractors' responsibility, not theirs!

Hershey's, like Nestlé, are facing legal action. Claims are they repeatedly abandon any serious attempt to address the issue of child labour in the production of their Hershey's Kisses, Kit Kat, Peppermint Patties and Reese's Peanut Butter Cups.

We can help these children by boycotting all the products mentioned above and by letting our friends on social media know what we are doing and why. There is nothing that brings a company to heel more than being named and shamed and nothing wakes up shareholders faster than a fall in their dividends.

> *'Child labor and poverty are inevitably bound together and if you continue to use the labor of children as the treatment for the social disease of poverty, you will have both poverty and child labor to the end of time.'*
>
> *Grace Abbott*

The effect of paternalism on birth control

As far back as 3000 BC, couples were experimenting with birth control. Fish bladders and animal intestines were often used as the forerunner of condoms. In the 1800s real condoms and the diaphragm appeared on the market. What was interesting in the US, the Comstock Act of 1873 prohibited the advertising and distribution of birth control and gave permission to the postal services to confiscate any birth control products that came through the mail.

A famous early advocate of birth control in the US was Margaret Sanger; she was probably the suffragette of the birth control movement. Sanger was prosecuted for writing a book, *Family Limitation*, which caused mayhem, and she had to flee to Britain until she felt it was safe to return.

She very bravely opened her first birth control clinic in 1916, leading to her arrest when an undercover policewoman purchased a copy of her information on family planning. Sanger believed it was a woman's right to determine when to bear children and to determine how many children she wanted to bear. She was desperate to prevent backstreet abortions, which caused the misery and death of so many young women. It wasn't until 1938 that a US judge lifted the ban on birth control, making it okay for women to use whatever birth control method they chose.

This is perhaps the most threatening shift of power for men;

women making their own birth control decisions for themselves is perhaps the ultimate slap in the face of paternalism.

Since becoming an adult, and in particular a woman working in the corporate world, I've experienced varying examples of paternalism. Men who treat women like bird-brains. Men who talk down to us. Men who patronise us. Men who clearly think being a man gives them rights to do and say whatever they want to regardless of appropriateness. And still in 2020, organisations think it's absolutely okay to pay a woman less than a man for doing the exact same job.

The word paternalism now suggests an implied power of superiority; a way to limit a person's liberty and freedom; a way to prevent women or children expressing opinions that differ from men in power, whether that be in a business sense, in government or in religion.

Men make the rules, women and children must follow them.

The English philosopher John Stuart Mill wrote a controversial essay, 'The Subjugation of Women', in 1869, which argues for equality between sexes, a concept that was met with derision by his fellow men, who believed such ideas were an 'affront to European conventional norms regarding the status of men and women'. In other words, men were superior to women. Mill went on to say that 'paternalism towards adults is sometimes thought of as treating them as if they were children' and I'd suggest that any woman who has experienced paternalism will tell you that is exactly what it feels like.

For example, when Saudi Arabia was considering allowing females to drive in 2017, a Saudi Arabian cleric claimed that women only have half a brain to begin with but when they go out shopping they end up with only a quarter. The cleric received a massive backlash on social media and was banned from preaching and leading prayers — the article doesn't say how long the ban lasted unfortunately.

The mature world should have been shocked at such an outrageous comment, and we were. However that very same year in the USA a raft of Republican senators gathered to debate healthcare under Trump and one of the items up for discussion was 'essential benefits including maternity services'. The horror was that there wasn't a single woman at the table. Once again, a backlash erupted. Jim McGovern, a Democratic senator, tweeted:

'This is outrageous: Not a single woman in the room as @Mike_Pence and @HouseGOP propose removing maternity coverage in #Trumpcare.'

The single most tragic aspect of Trump's presidency has been his attaching himself to the evangelicals. My grandmother famously said 'Never trust a man with a Bible'. For some, religion and their book of choice offers and gives comfort; for others, it provides a rigid set of rules, mostly, it would appear, a set of rules to keep women in line.

Top of the evangelical political agenda appears to be removing a woman's right to terminations. Together with the GOP they are doing everything they can to defund 'Planned Parenthood', the very thing women need access to in order *not* to get pregnant.

If women are to prevent unwanted pregnancies they need access to safe and affordable birth control yet it would appear that everything is being set up to make birth control options less available. When the inevitable happens and the woman (or girl) finds herself pregnant, then the wrath of God is put firmly on her head for letting herself get pregnant. As far as I know, getting pregnant takes two people, a man and a woman.

The curious thing is that once that possibly unwanted child is born, the self-same Republicans and evangelicals want nothing more to do with a living breathing child. It would appear the only thing they care about is the foetus. Do they really care about the foetus or is it rather the loss of control of women they fear?

Abortion is a massively emotional issue but for quite some time there have been common-sense laws about ending a pregnancy: rape, incest, age and health of the mother are all pretty humane reasons for making it okay.

Alabama Governor Kay Ivey recently signed into law a bill that bans nearly all abortions, even in the case of rape and incest. The law throws out all humanity. The view of the people behind the law is that 'We understand that issues like rape and incest are difficult topics to tackle; nevertheless, it is our view that the value of human life is not determined by the circumstances of one's conception or birth.' This group also advocates that any doctor who performs a termination should go to prison for 99 years. Fortunately, at time of writing, these laws have not been passed.

So desperate women will do what they've done for centuries when faced with an unwanted pregnancy: they will risk their lives by using whatever means at their disposal to end that pregnancy.

Argentina rejected a bill that would have decriminalised terminations in the first 14 weeks of pregnancy; a week later a 34-year-old woman died from septic shock when she tried a self-termination using parsley. One doctor said that 'Illegality forces the poorest women to use the most desperate practices.'

In America the stacking of the Supreme Court with conservative Republicans like Brett Kavanaugh appears to be part of a covert and deliberate strategy to overthrow Roe v. Wade: the US Supreme Court ruling that 'The Constitution of the United States protects a pregnant woman's liberty to choose to have an abortion without excessive government restriction'.

Roe v. Wade has been credited with what we now see as the great divide between pro-life and pro-choice advocates in America.

According to the Guttmacher Institute, approximately 8–11% of maternal deaths are down to botched terminations.

The World Health Organization discovered that between 2010 and 2014 around 56 million safe and unsafe terminations occurred worldwide; that 25 million unsafe terminations are estimated to take place each year, mostly in developing countries. Yet all these terminations could be prevented with access to good sex education, effectively priced birth control and access to safe terminations; and surely with a population already at 7.5 billion people, surely finding ways to limit family size is pure common sense.

Richard Nixon, a Republican president, for all his faults had set in place a promise that no American woman should be denied access to family planning because of her financial situation. His programme was called Title X. What the Trump administration has tried to do is imply that Title X helps women abort pregnancies, but it doesn't. Title X was set up to subsidise birth control, to facilitate STD screening and other reproductive health services for low-income families who probably couldn't afford healthcare.

In my experience, I've met only a few women who have elected to have a pregnancy terminated. Their reasons varied but the end result didn't — not a single woman ever got over the decision. They live with the guilt and pain for the rest of their lives.

Ireland, a predominantly Roman Catholic country, surprised the whole world in 2018 by permitting terminations during the first 12 weeks of pregnancy and later in the case of health issues for the mother or foetal abnormalities. Some countries still force girls and women who have been raped and fall pregnant to marry their rapist.

The question is — who owns a woman's body? Surely a woman owns her body?

I guess it would have been no great surprise hearing a man in Saudi talk about the size of a woman's brain or whether women are sensible enough to drive a car, or to have a whole raft of GOP men discuss women's reproductive rights in the year 1820, but 2020 — really? Paternalism gone bonkers. Don't they have bigger and better things to worry about than our reproductive systems? We are quite capable of looking after this ourselves, thanks, guys.

> *'Worse, they suggested this was a considerate move for the protection of women, conveniently disguising their discrimination with a thin veneer of patronizing gallantry.'*
>
> *Qanta A. Ahmed, In the Land of Invisible Women: A female doctor's journey in the Saudi kingdom*

What being a conservative really means and why most women find it offensive

Definition: Conservatism is a commitment to traditional values and ideas with opposition to change or innovation. The holding of political views that favour free enterprise, private ownership, and socially conservative ideas.

In 2004, Philip E. Agre wrote an article asking 'What is conservatism?' and 'What is wrong with conservatism?' and gave his own answers:

Q: What is conservatism?

A: Conservatism is the domination of society by an aristocracy.

Q: What is wrong with conservatism?

A: Conservatism is incompatible with democracy, prosperity, and civilization in general. It is a destructive system of inequality and prejudice that is founded on deception and has no place in the modern world.

Agre goes on to say: 'From the pharaohs of ancient Egypt to the self-regarding thugs of ancient Rome to the glorified warlords of medieval and absolutist Europe, in nearly every urbanized society throughout human history, there have been people who have tried to constitute themselves as an aristocracy. These people and their allies are the conservatives. The tactics of conservatism vary widely by place and time. But the most central feature of conservatism is deference: a psychologically internalized attitude on the part of the common people that the aristocracy are better people than they are.'

> *'Deregulation is a transfer of power from the trodden to the treading. It is unsurprising that all conservative parties claim to hate big government.'*
>
> *George Monbiot*

Why are older white men suddenly so angry?

As we've already seen, men have been the 'authority' for thousands of years: head of the family, leaders in the church, leaders in business and banking, leaders in the community. For hundreds if not thousands of years, they made the rules and women and children were expected to follow them.

In business or the church or society, when things have been done the way they've been done for however many years, doing things differently is utterly terrifying for most people and being told you must do things differently can cause hackles to rise.

Now in the third decade of the 21st century, little by little, inch by inch, qualification by qualification, women are breaking the glass ceilings in all manner of ways. When they get into the boardroom they ask questions like 'Why do we do it that way?', 'Have you thought about doing it a different way?', 'How will doing it that way affect our employees, our customers, our communities?'

How annoying we women are.

Men's anger caused one researcher to try to explain their vitriolic reaction. Camilla Nelson, an Associate Professor in Media at the University of Notre Dame, suggested that 'Greta Thunberg scares some men silly' and that the 'bullying of a teenager by conservative middle-aged men has taken on a grim, almost hysterical edge'. Her deduction is that they are 'reaching deep into the misogynist's playbook to divert focus from her message'.

Male beratement of vocal women isn't new. As we've already seen, the medical profession have labelled such women as needing medication or bed rest or hospitalisation if they dare to raise their voices or express anger.

I was delighted when Scott Morrison, the Australian prime minister, stepped in to support Jacinda Ardern immediately after the Christchurch massacre, but was shocked when he suggested that 'women's advancement should not come at the expense of men'. He said this on International Women's Day 2019. Morrison received a swift response from Australia's Shadow Minister for Women, Tanya Plibersek, who suggested that gender equality is 'good for both women and men. It gives all of us more freedom and choice at work, at home, and in our relationships. Feminism is a fight for equality between men and women, what's so complicated about that?'

Scott Morrison also suggested that the climate change debate was subjecting Australian children to 'needless anxiety; we've got to let kids be kids'. He believes that 'the public debate was replete with disinformation about Australia's climate change policies'. Yet even as I wrote this chapter, Australia was on fire and was recently recorded as the hottest place on the planet; Venice was under water, and many of the Pacific Islands are simply vanishing under rising sea levels.

We are fighting to save the planet *for* our children!

Every now and then I post something about climate change on LinkedIn and I can pretty much guarantee that the negative reactions I get will be from older white men. I've been staggered at the reaction of these same older men to Greta Thunberg and Jacinda Ardern. It was discovered here in New Zealand that one sad old man goes around all the bookshops and magazine outlets in his local area and if he sees a picture of Jacinda anywhere, he turns her face around.

That takes sad to a whole new level.

It's fair to say that most people don't like change; or is it that they don't like being told they need to change?

Do men view this rising of the female population, from Greta to Jacinda, from Jane Fonda to the #MeToo movement, as signs that we women are getting above our station? Why was it that it seemed to be mostly women leading the marches for the environment, and young people who were the ones standing up to the likes of the NRA?

So, as is my wont, I asked the question on Google: 'Why are white men so angry?'

According to Wikipedia, 'angry white male' is a pejorative expression for white males holding conservative to reactionary views in the context of US politics; typically characterised by 'opposition to liberal anti-discriminatory policies and beliefs in particular in opposition to some affirmative action policies and modern feminism'.

This reaction is not limited to the USA or New Zealand. Angry white men appeared in the Australian 1998 federal elections. New political parties appeared concerned for 'fathers' rights', and included the Abolish Family Support/Family Court Party and the Family Law Reform Party, both parties vehemently opposing what they saw as a feminist agenda. They believe that 'feminists have entrenched themselves into positions of power and influence' and are 'using their power to victimise men'.

Which begs the question, are men actually afraid of women?

Most women, in my experience, simply have points of view that may differ from their male counterparts; not better, just different. Can we not work together as equals versus being seen as threats? Are male egos so fragile that men can't bear to be questioned or challenged? Are they so entrenched in 'this is the way it has always been done' that they feel personally threatened if someone suggests a different way?

Does it mean that women are always right? Of course not, it just means that anyone should be able to ask a question, young or old, male or female, white or non-white. It's called inclusion; it's called listening; it's called considering all options.

In my experience, the more people are listened to and involved in decision-making, the more valued they feel and the better decisions we make in the long run. White men don't have all the answers and as we look at some of the cultures that still treat their women worse than the family donkey, non-white men don't have the answers either.

Surely the world is facing bigger issues than men versus women? Isn't working together to solve problems the logical solution? Together we can perhaps ensure there is a planet for our children, grandchildren and their grandchildren. Perhaps some men just need to get over themselves?

> *'I myself have never been able to find out precisely what feminism is: I only know that people call me a feminist whenever I express sentiments that differentiate me from a doormat.'*
>
> *Rebecca West*

Men who champion women

If you are still with me, I hope you get it that this book really isn't a tirade about all men. I know there are thousands of good guys out there, and more and more of them are showing up and supporting women's rights. More and more of them are realising that we really can't keep doing what we've always done now the planet is in peril; and if things have to be done differently, so what? If it is women who call out the hypocrisy, so what?

If you've seen President Obama with his wife and daughters, it's obvious that he is a man who is not threatened by women in any way, shape or form. He said: 'Most people who meet my wife quickly conclude that she is remarkable. They are right about this. She is smart, funny and thoroughly charming. Often, after hearing her speak at some function or working with her on a project, people will approach me and say something to the effect of, you know, I think the world of you, Barack, but your wife, wow!'

William Golding said: 'I think women are foolish to pretend they are equal to men; they are far superior and always have been.' Daniel Craig believes that 'Women are responsible for two-thirds of the work done worldwide yet earn only ten percent of the total income and own one percent of the property.'

So, are we equals? Until the answer is yes, we must never stop asking and we must never stop challenging.

Actor Benedict Cumberbatch has pledged to take on only roles where his female co-stars receive the same salary he does. Emma Stone shared the fact that her male co-stars have taken salary cuts so that she received equal pay. Harry Belafonte shared his experience as a civil rights activist when he marched with Martin Luther King Jr in the 1960s, and helped as an adviser to the women who were organising the Women's March, to protest the inauguration of Trump. Sir Ian McKellen and Jake Gyllenhaal were part of that women's march.

After John Legend became father to a daughter, he stated quite clearly that men shouldn't wait until they have daughters to become aware of how women are treated. He said: 'It doesn't cost us anything as men, for women to do well. We don't lose out because more women are empowered … more women are leaders. It just makes the world better.'

Ashton Kutcher is another vocal advocate for gender equality, and actor David Schwimmer (Ross Geller on *Friends*) created a series of short films based on real incidents of workplace sexual harassment as part of a campaign called #ThatsHarassment. He wanted to encourage people to speak out if they were victims of harassment. He acknowledges that bullying and harassment is about 'power' or, more particularly, the abuse of power.

So as more male role models step us and say enough alongside the women who are saying enough, hopefully before too long we should see a seismic shift in equality on all fronts for women.

> *'The world will be saved by Western women. Not any women, perhaps not all women, but Burning Women. Women who have stepped out of silence and into the fullness of their power. Angry women who love the world and her creatures too much to let it be destroyed so thoughtlessly for a moment longer.'*
>
> *The Dalai Lama*

Questions regarding Chapter 3

Did anything in this chapter surprise you?

Did any aspect of the chapter irritate you, concern you or even make you feel angry?

Is it your belief that men should maintain their hold on power?

Does understanding what 'conservatism' is make you think differently in any way?

Do you have men in your life who believe that 'women should know their place'?

In what ways have you experienced paternalism?

How did/does that make you feel?

Do you express those feelings?

What are your feelings around a woman's right to make decisions about her own body?

What was your reaction when you read that the Dalai Lama suggests that it is women who will save the world?

Does that surprise you or fill you with energy?

4

WHY DOING WHAT WE'VE ALWAYS DONE NO LONGER WORKS

'The significant problems we face cannot be solved at the same level of thinking we were at when we created them.'

Einstein

Understanding feminism

Definition: Feminism is a range of social movements, political movements and ideologies that aim to define, establish and achieve political, economic, personal and social equality of the sexes.

Which brings us back to the dreaded word 'feminist'.

Rebecca West, writing for *Good Housekeeping* (hardly a rebellious magazine), said: 'When many women hear the word "feminism", they think about angry, bra-burning ladies in the 1970s, terms like "man-hater" and worse. But these days, a feminist isn't someone who hates men, and it isn't even necessarily someone who identifies as a woman. Anyone can be a feminist, and you don't have to be politically active to support the cause.'

Being a feminist simply means believing that women and men should have the same opportunities; the same pay for doing the same job, the same rights to run for office, the same opportunity to be the boss, and the right to say no to inappropriate advances without fear of recrimination.

Surely any father reading this book would want this for his daughters?

Having spent most of my life in personnel and human resource roles, I was horribly familiar with advertising jobs that had one pay rate for men and another for women — for doing the same job! There was a time when you could actually advertise those differentials; now all it means is that the differentials have gone to ground but rest assured the interviewer will have two rates in mind when going through the selection process.

It used to irritate the heck out of me. I would challenge this practice at every opportunity only to be met with the 'men have families to support' argument. Tosh. There are so many women now bringing up children on their own for whatever reason, so that argument simply doesn't hold water any longer. I'd always believed, price the job. Whatever the job is, whoever does it, this is the rate.

We've already met some of those early feminists in the suffragettes.

In the 19th and early 20th centuries, women fought not just for the right to vote but for equal rights in marriage and property ownership. At that stage only men could own property and if a woman came into a marriage as a property owner, her property was now owned by her husband. If the marriage failed, she walked away with nothing, even having to leave her children behind.

A second wave of feminism swept the world in the early 1960s when people like Gloria Steinem became a renowned social and political activist. A columnist for the *New York* magazine, she co-founded *Ms.* magazine and published the article 'After Black Power, Women's Liberation'.

Steinem's mother had a mental breakdown at the age of 34 which left her an invalid. Her father was a travelling salesman, so a 10-year-old Steinem pretty much became her mother's caregiver. Eventually the marriage failed and although Steinem didn't blame her father for walking away, she did become aggrieved at the way her mother was treated when she tried to find work and the apathetic way the medical system treated her. These formative years built into her a determination to tackle the social injustices women faced on a daily basis.

The tragedy for women is that if they declare they are a feminist, the label brings all manner of negative connotations, the assumption being that if you are a feminist you must hate men. So very rarely do women come out and proudly say 'I am a feminist'. Yet ask them if they believe it is fair that men and women are paid differently for doing the exact same job or do they think it fair that women's property should be handed over to their husband once they are married and they will state that it is categorically *not* okay.

The famous story of the Dagenham women workers who went on strike at the local Ford Motor Company in 1968 was eventually made into a movie. The misconception is that they went on strike for equal pay when in fact that wasn't the case; they went on strike because of the company's refusal to upgrade them to a skill level that gave them a pay increase. Men could be upgraded, but women were never upgraded.

The 187 women who downed tools were machinists responsible for making the seat covers for Ford cars. They were categorised as 'B' grade workers — in other words they were classed as unskilled workers. What really offended them was that they even received less pay than men who simply swept the floors. Even doing these lowly jobs, men were also classed as 'B' grade workers and received a higher pay rate than the women. Not even their union supported them in their fight for acknowledgement. The union felt that the fees these 187 female workers paid weren't worth the union's trouble. The women went on strike. No seat covers were made. You can't sell cars without seat covers!

So here is a feminism test: Try mentioning the word 'feminism' in a group of men and women and watch the reactions. Not just from men who scorn the word but from women who also seem to be threatened by the concept. Then ask them if they think it is fair that women are paid less for doing exactly the same job as a man.

> *'When a man gives his opinion, he's a man; when a woman gives her opinion, she's a bitch.'*
>
> *Bette Davis*

Is this all there is?

As wives and mothers and even as grandmothers, most women, as they load the dishwasher, prepare the meals, organise school uniforms, etc., must think 'Is this all there is?' Where did my dream of becoming a writer or a jazz singer or an airline pilot go?

We probably still take on the bulk of household chores. We still seem to be the ones who have to remember everyone's birthdays and to do all the shopping for cards and gifts. I still believe the majority of us are the ones that do the dirtiest jobs — cleaning the toilet, changing nappies, tending to whichever child is throwing up his/her lunch, wiping the runny noses alongside and at the same time as dealing with that near-fatal dose of man-flu.

I would hope that most of us in 2020 have partners who share the workload as we women try to juggle work and family. A Canadian study conducted in 2017 found that not to be the case. Their summary was that 'Women of all ages still tend to do more household chores than their male partners, no matter how much they work or earn in a job outside the home.'

The researchers collected data from 900+ Canadians from high school to the workplace and then from adolescence into adulthood. They examined how household tasks were divided between individuals and their partners and 'how housework was influenced by one's work hours, relative income, marital status and responsibilities towards children'.

The research also established that the party in the relationship with the lowest income tended to be the one who bore the burden of housework and that gender played the biggest predictor of who did what.

The study hopes that policymakers and employers will factor in the results of the study to 'alter laws, policies and work environments that promote men's involvement in unpaid labour'.

'When men say they help around the house it usually means "I once put a wet towel in the laundry basket".'

Not known (probably a woman sick of picking up wet towels.)

Why it's okay for women to acknowledge their own anger

I'd gone through years of counselling after the abuse by my stepfather and I truly thought I was sorted, cured, healed. I was getting on with my life; I had a fabulous career, I was now in a long-term relationship with a man I really cared about, and both my kids were doing well. I had beautiful grandchildren and my new husband and I had just built a gorgeous home near the beach. Life was good.

And then Donald Trump, who from this page forward shall be known as HWSBN (he-who-shall-be-nameless), came down the escalator.

Everything I thought I'd dealt with as a child rose to the surface again. If I could have been waiting at the bottom of the escalator on that fateful day, I think I would have beaten him to a pulp with my bare hands. How dare he run for POTUS especially after we had experienced such an amazing man when Obama was president? When did it become okay for a serial womaniser and a serial bankrupt to even enter the fray? Surely there should be some pretty tight criteria for giving someone access to the nuclear codes?

For the next three years I was seriously angry that this odious man took over from President Obama, a man of grace and dignity. I called HWSBN out on Facebook every day; I wrote two books about him and still I was angry.

My friends kept telling me to chill. To move on. To let it go. But I couldn't.

I tried self-talk:

'You're not really angry, you are concerned.' 'No, I'm angry.'

'You're not really angry, you are scared.' 'No, I'm angry.'

Nothing eased the rage inside. Writing the two books helped a bit; raging on Facebook alongside others who were as concerned as I was helped. I learned to deal with all manner of 'others' — the people who adored him and could see nothing wrong with the terrible things he said and the horrible things he did.

I felt as if I could see a massive tidal wave on the horizon and I was frantically trying to alert people about the danger and they just didn't want to know. I just couldn't believe it.

I came at my anger from a different angle because I needed to; people were starting to look at me as if I was some sort of mad woman. I researched what anger *is*; and in particular, I looked into why it seems to be okay for men to get angry but not okay for women.

The *Encyclopedia of Psychology* describes anger as 'an emotion characterized by antagonism toward someone or something you feel has deliberately done you wrong'. It goes on to say that 'anger can be a good thing, it can give you a way to express negative feelings, for example, or motivate you to find solutions to problems', however, it cautions that 'excessive anger can cause health problems'.

I was certainly dealing with blood pressure issues. I was waking several times a night battling with this odious man as every day he seemed to get worse. His bullying and name-calling drove me nuts. His need to undo everything Obama had put in place, in particular all the environmental protections, made my hair stand on end. My rage was making it difficult for me to think straight. Every day I was outraged at the things he said, the way he treated people and the never-ending lies he told, even when he didn't need to lie.

We are frequently told that anger doesn't hurt the other person, it only hurts us, which doesn't help when you don't know what to do with the anger. I actually understood the root cause of my anger: a hideous stepfather. My challenge was harnessing the harmful energy and putting it into a positive framework. I knew absolutely that my physical and mental health were being adversely affected, and I also knew that the concern my friends and family were feeling for me was actually justified.

Undeterred, I continued my exploration of what anger is for us as women, and what use it is, if any. I discovered an article that suggested there were three types of anger:

1. Passive aggression (the 'poor me' syndrome interspersed with bouts of loud rage)
2. Open aggression (pure and simple loud rage)
3. Assertive anger (productive action as a result of the feelings).

Back to more self-talk:

'You're not angry, you are feeling a sense of injustice.' 'You're right, I am feeling that.'

'You're not feeling angry, you are feeling powerless.' 'Ah, you are so right, that's exactly what this is about for me. Got it.'

I was powerless as a 10-year-old being abused by a stepfather. Seeing HWSBN coming down that escalator brought my sense of powerlessness back to the surface with a vengeance. But I wasn't a 10-year-old now, I was a feisty grandmother and I needed to turn that negative energy into positive behaviours before I had a stroke or someone sent for the little white van to cart me away.

So I did. I followed up the first two HWSBN books with *this* one, and I felt so much better.

Leslie Jamison, in an article called 'I used to insist I didn't get angry. Not anymore', suggests that 'If an angry woman makes people uneasy, then her more palatable counterpart, the sad woman, summons sympathy more readily. She often looks beautiful in her suffering: ennobled, transfigured, elegant. Angry women are messier. Their pain threatens to cause more collateral damage. It's as if the prospect of a woman's anger harming other people threatens to rob her of the social capital she has gained by being wronged.'

Jamison on Hillary Clinton: 'In *What Happened,* ... Clinton describes the pressure not to come across as angry during the course of her entire political career — "a lot of people recoil from an angry woman".'

Post her election loss, Clinton talked about how hard it was to keep her cool that day in the debates when HWSBN was pacing behind her, invading her space, intimidating her in whatever way he could. She imagined what would have happened if she had stood up to him right there and then. Imagine that? The tragedy for her on that occasion was that she was damned if she did call him out and damned if she didn't. She did the only thing she could do: she ignored him.

We must remember that we women are not powerless; we are incredibly powerful once we learn how to tap into that power and energy and use it in a way that isn't destructive to ourselves and will be productive for others.

Who can ever forget the sheer number of women who had won seats and then wore white as they were inducted into American politics after the 2018 mid-term elections? These women were mobilised by their anger and determination to deal to the man in the Oval Office.

'Before, if you were to ask me why I was crying, I would probably tell you that I was sad or tired. It turns out, more often than not, I was tired and angry and specifically, tired of being angry. If I cry, people are more likely to respond to me with kindness, or at least, to respond at all. They are less likely to fire me, deny me a raise, ignore my police report, forget to write down my illness symptoms, or threaten me with physical violence. Even if I say "I am angry at you" in my calmest and softest voice, I am still likely to be met with fear, anger, and resentment. I am in the process of opening up to my own anger instead of going to extreme lengths to avoid or hold the anger of others.'

Leslie Jamison

Young women fearlessly saying 'ENOUGH!'

The #MeToo movement woke up the next generation of women and heralded in the third wave of feminism. Hallelujah. We now have a breed of young women who feel no fear at expressing their rage, their fury, their angst. Good on them.

I picked up an article called 'In the 2010s, Celebrity Feminism Got Trendy. Then Women Got Angry'. Taylor Swift's latest album, *Speak Now*, echoes her introduction to and rage at the various shades of inequality women in any workplace still experience. When asked if she classed herself a feminist she replied, 'I've never really thought about that.' And so the question was raised with many other famous women: Beyoncé, Lorde, Katy Perry and Susan Sarandon.

Caitlin Lawson, a post-doctoral fellow in communication and media at the University of Michigan, said: 'I think into the decade, there was this rising popularity of feminism that started off as a slow burn and then increased toward the middle of the decade.' In 2012, Nigerian author Chimamanda Ngozi Adichie said in a TED talk that 'we should all be feminists'.

So if you are a woman reading this and just slightly suspect you too are a feminist or fast becoming one, then be proud of that.

We could in fact credit HWSBN with awakening women. It appears I was not the only one that was angry after his election. Stars like Beyoncé and Katy Perry have millions and millions of followers, their opinions matter. They can take a whole new generation of women into a world where *their* opinions matter and this new generation will speak up.

Being 'ladylike' holds no sway for them. Thank goodness.

> *'What people don't realise about Donald Trump — and I don't know if Donald Trump realises it — is that every tweet he unleashes against you ... creates such a crescendo of anger.'*
>
> *Megyn Kelly*

Questions regarding Chapter 4

Would you describe yourself as a feminist?

If you are happy being a feminist, how does that manifest?

If you wouldn't describe yourself as a feminist, are you okay with women being paid less to do the same job as a man?

Do you have days when you think 'Is this all there is?'?

In your household, who does the 'dirty' jobs?

Do you have times when you feel really angry?

How do you express that?

Are you a 'yeller', or do you stifle those feelings?

Have you found a way to say 'That isn't okay for me' or 'That doesn't sit well with me'?

If you say you are not happy with something, how do the people around you react?

Are you comfortable stating your case and not feeling the need to make the other person feel 'okay'?

Do you envy the fact that young women have no fear of speaking up?

How would your life be different if you did the same?

5

GREED IS NOT GOOD

'Greed, in the end, fails even the greedy.'

Cathryn Louis

Why capitalism is killing us all

Definition: Capitalism is an economic system in which the means of production and distribution are privately or corporately owned and the operations are funded by profits. An example of capitalism is the prison system in the United States being operated by private companies.

I've been in the workplace long enough to remember sensible CEO and managerial salaries. The wage and salary gap has always been a bone of contention, but never more so than now. When we read about the massive salary packages of current CEOs, it makes no sense at all. No-one is worth the kind of money that is being bandied around, surely?

When did it all go awry? Who decided that someone was worth making more money in an hour than most families make in a year?

Steve Denning, writing for *Forbes,* agreed with Jack Welch, the former CEO of GE, that maximising shareholder investment was 'the world's dumbest idea'. Two Harvard Business School professors, Joseph L. Bower and Lynn S. Paine, deduced that the idea of putting shareholders first is 'flawed in its assumptions, confused as a matter of law, and damaging in practice'. They even called the idea 'pernicious nonsense'.

Jack Welch had always believed that customers, employees and a quality product should be a company's most important focus. He felt sure that shareholders wanting fast returns encouraged owners and managers to make short-term decisions; decisions that in the long run could cost everyone.

And so it was this shift that started the lunacy of CEOs being paid obscene salaries and employees being kept on the least wage possible for as long as possible. When a family needs two or even three jobs just to provide the basics for their family, something has gone horribly wrong.

Short-term thinking in any business has all manner of risks. *The Economist* suggests that when all that matters in an organisation is shareholder value, then owners and managers are given a 'license for bad conduct, including skimping on investment, exorbitant pay, high leverage, silly takeovers, accounting shenanigans and a craze for share buy-backs'.

So whose dumb idea was it anyway?

> *'In the 1980s came the paroxysm of downsizing, and the very nature of the corporation was thrown into doubt. In what began almost as a fad and quickly matured into an unshakable habit, companies were "restructuring", "reengineering", and generally cutting as many jobs as possible, white collar as well as blue ... The New York Times captured the new corporate order succinctly in 1987, reporting that it "eschews loyalty to workers, products, corporate structures, businesses, factories, communities, even the nation. All such allegiances are viewed as expendable under the new rules".'*
>
> *Barbara Ehrenreich*

Blame it on Milton Friedman

In his 1962 book *Capitalism and Freedom*, Friedman declared that 'there is one and only one social responsibility of business—to use its resources and engage in activities designed to increase its profits'. This gave CEOs freedom to focus only on profits and to give no regard to 'costs'. Costs to families, costs to communities and costs to the environment.

So he is the one who caused this nightmare.

We were also sold the delusion that this radical new system would eventually 'trickle down' and everyone would benefit.

So if focusing only on shareholder profits was the dumbest idea ever, trickle-down economics was the biggest lie ever.

> *'If one feeds the horse enough oats, some will pass through to the road for the sparrows.'*
>
> *John Galbraith*

Ending the rape and pillage

It has surely taken a while, but finally the realisation is that 'shareholder only' thinking is not healthy for workers, for their families, for communities, and is absolutely devastating to the environment. Yes, some people have ended up becoming incredibly wealthy, but 99% of the world's population have not benefited by one red cent.

Hopefully, sanity is returning.

Apparently, 200 corporate CEOs including of Apple, Amazon and Walmart took out a full-page ad in the *New York Times* to say they are redefining the purpose of a corporation.

Given that Apple, Amazon and Walmart appear in my next chapter as shamefully unethical companies, I read this with some scepticism. These are the companies that were given the massive tax breaks under Trump and to date not much of that has trickled down to their employees; most of these organisations used the money to simply buy back shares.

During their discussion on what the purpose of a corporation should be, they discovered that the challenge wasn't in recognising that change was required, their confusion was how to implement such change.

Really?

Call me old-fashioned, but perhaps the first step would be to pay their people a living wage and the second step would be to pay a fair share of country taxes?

Research has gone on for some years with input from Mars, Incorporated; Oxford University; the Paris School of Economics; the Sorbonne; CEIBS in China; and ENSEA in Côte d'Ivoire to develop innovative solutions for more corporate responsibility. Their conclusion was a system they have labelled the Economics of Mutuality (EoM), innovation that equips leaders with practical business tools to solve the problems of people, planet and profitability.

Their research also discredits the belief that human, social and environmental value will come at the expense of profits.

Any worker could have told them that.

> *'Our social capital is now badly depleted. This erosion manifests in the weakened norms of behavior that once restrained the most selfish impulses of economic actors and provided an ethical basis for modern capitalism. A capitalism in which Wall Street bankers and traders think peddling dangerous loans or worthless securities to unsuspecting customers is just 'part of the game', a capitalism in which top executives believe it is economically necessary that they earn 350 times what their front-line workers do, a capitalism that thinks of employees as expendable inputs, a capitalism in which corporations perceive it as both their fiduciary duty to evade taxes and their constitutional right to use unlimited amounts of corporate funds to purchase control of the political system—that is a capitalism whose trust deficit is every bit as corrosive as budget and trade deficits.'*
>
> *Steven Pearlstein*

At the very least, let's get ethical

Ethical Consumer names and shames some of the worst corporates for 2018 as being:

Nestlé

Monsanto

Amazon

Tesco

Walmart.

According to their research, all these companies rate poorly over a number of rankings: human rights, animal rights, and environmental concerns.

Nestlé: The company has been subject to the world's longest-running boycott for the irresponsible marketing of baby milk to mothers in the developing world; the use of unsustainable palm oil; and for using genetically modified ingredients in its foods.

Caroline Winter of *Bloomsberg Businessweek* visited the Nestlé bottling plant in Michigan to investigate the corporation's practice of promising much needed jobs to small communities when their real goal is to buy up public land to gain control of water rights.

I guess most people would be unaware that in 2019 Nestlé sold US$7.7 billion worth of bottled water making it the world's largest bottled water company. It pays the US Forest Service only US$524 a year to draw 30 million gallons of public water in San Bernardino, California. It pays the city of Evart, Michigan just US$250,000 a year for its water.

What the whole world is witnessing is a slow move towards the privatisation of water. Multinational corporations don't have the public's best interests in mind, they have shareholder profits in mind. Peter Brabeck-Letmathe, Nestlé's recently retired CEO, declared that 'water is not a human right'.

Ethical Consumer recommended alternatives: Plamil chocolate

and Divine Chocolate; and here in Australia and New Zealand I fully recommend Whittaker's chocolate.

Monsanto has actually been described as the most evil corporation on earth. It was founded by John Francis Queeny, a member of the Knights of Malta. Its very first product was dangerous. The company developed chemical saccharin and sold it to Coca-Cola as an artificial sweetener knowing full well that the product was poisonous.

Undaunted, in the 1920s it moved full swing into PCBs (polychlorinated biphenyls). Initially, PCBs were thought of as a wonder chemical, an oil that wouldn't burn, would never degrade and would have almost limitless uses. PCBs have been implicated in reproductive, developmental and immune system disorders. Even now, after being banned for 50 years for causing such devastation, the chemical is still present in most animal products, human blood and tissue cells across the globe. The worst part is that during court trials to ban the product, documentation showed that Monsanto knew full well about the deadly effects but chose to hide this information from the public.

In the 1930s the company developed its first hybrid seed corn and expanded into detergents, soaps, industrial cleaning products, synthetic rubbers and plastics; all toxic.

In the 1940s it was the company that began research into uranium, which was used in the bombs dropped on Hiroshima and Nagasaki, killing hundreds of thousands of people.

In the 1960s, Monsanto, along with Dow Chemical, produced Agent Orange for use in the US's Vietnam invasion. Over three million people were contaminated, a half million Vietnamese civilians dead, a half-million Vietnamese babies born with birth defects, and thousands of US military veterans continuing to suffer and die from the effects.

It would seem that from the day the company was first launched, it would have known full well that its products were not only harmful but deadly. Its response in a 2002 trial where evidence proved beyond doubt that its products presented dangers to people and the environment was:

'Where do we go from here? The alternatives: go out of business; sell the hell out of them as long as we can and do nothing else; try to stay in business; have alternative products.'

Amazon is owned by the richest man in the world, Jeff Bezos, a man who pays no taxes and donates nothing to charity. The company is well known for terrible treatment of its workers, for lack of care over safety issues and for even less care for any area when they build yet another of their outlets.

A *Guardian* investigation revealed 'numerous cases where Amazon workers are left to suffer after sustaining workplace injuries, leaving them unable to work, deprived of income, and forced to fight for months to receive benefits and medical care'.

The ideal city for them to build new offices and warehouses would have 'more than a million people, mass transit, an international airport, attractive housing and "stable and business-friendly" regulations'.

For 'business-friendly' read turning a blind eye to worker rights, safety regulations and environmental protection. The company refuses to release any data on its environmental policy or use of greenhouse gases. Environmentalists rank it as one of the least transparent corporations for its size.

Ethical Consumer recommends alternatives to dealing with Amazon:

Oxfam books

Better World Books

Hive.

TESCO was investigated by the Serious Fraud Office in 2014 after a whistle-blower brought to light suspicious accounting practices. It was discovered that desperate executives were doing some creative accounting with supplier payments; pulling payments forward to paint a more favourable bottom line.

After the investigation eight senior executives including the head of the UK food group were dismissed and bonus payments to other senior executives were withheld as the investigations continued.

Ethical Consumer suggests that this investigation is just one aspect of what have always been questionable ethics at the company.

Best Buy alternatives:

Marks & Spencer

Co-op

Waitrose (online).

Coca-Cola is another company with a long history of violating worker rights. The company also has a poor record on sustainability and the environment, having been 'accused of taking water supplies from rural communities and falsifying environmental data'.

Best Buy alternatives:

ChariTea

Lemonaid.

Walmart: As a result of the Trump tax cuts to corporates, Walmart received benefits to the tune of US$6.5 billion. That equates to US$1.1 million a day in tax breaks. Meanwhile, its employees make an average of US$19,177 per annum and many workers rely on a government top-up to make ends meet. This government top-up to Walmart and McDonald's alone costs the American taxpayers US$153 billion in public assistance.

Somewhere we've lost the plot.

As if wages versus owner wealth wasn't a glaring issue, Walmart's record of supplier treatment and abuse of worker rights is well known. Abuses appear to happen at all levels of the organisation from suppliers and factory safety to environmental issues and discrimination.

In a 2017 article by Alexander Kaufman it appears that a group of workers bandied together and bought some Walmart shares; enough shares that would allow them to submit resolutions. Their suggestion was to put an environmental expert on the board so that Walmart couldn't continue paying lip service to environmental issues. Walmart's response to the suggest was that it believed that its charity work was sufficient to offset environmental issues.

Rob Walton serves on the board of directors of Conservation International, a non-profit organisation to which Walmart has donated millions but which critics say is basically a 'greenwashing' campaign. Walton is also co-chair of the Arizona State University Global Institute of Sustainability, to which the family foundation gave US$27 million in 2012.

It would seem that giving money possibly assuages their guilt, sadly it doesn't do anything for their staff or the communities they trade in and absolutely nothing for the environment.

According to Kaufman, 'for a retail behemoth whose business model still depends heavily on pollution, Walmart's green policies are more akin to a face-lift than surgical reconstruction'.

Best Buy alternatives:

Co-op

Marks & Spencer

Waitrose (online).

I'd like to add two more organisations to this list of bad eggs:

Modelez: This a company you may never have heard of, but which was called out in a 2018 article by Jane Dalton writing for the *Independent*. Modelez is one of the world's largest purchasers of palm oil, which is used in Cadbury, Oreo, and Ritz crackers. It continues to decimate tens of thousands of hectares of orangutan habitat. Future generations would surely prefer these beautiful creatures to chocolate. Greenpeace campaigners warn 'it's now or never for Indonesia's critically endangered orangutans, which are being killed at a rate of 25 a day as natural vegetation is bulldozed to make way for palm plantations'.

The Red Cross and Oxfam: In late 2010, Haiti was struck by a massive earthquake. It was already a desperately poor area, and homes were built with all manner of materials, none of which were meant to withstand an earthquake. Haiti was pretty much flattened. The Red Cross launched a multi-million-dollar fundraising initiative with the intention of rebuilding Haiti. Half a billion dollars was eventually raised.

The Red Cross claims it has provided homes to more than 130,000 people, but the actual number of permanent homes the group has built in all of Haiti is six.

Where did US$500 million in donations go?

It would appear that the Red Cross took out quite a sizeable chunk of money for their own admin costs. They gave money to a variety of organisations to effect the rebuild and then these organisations took out money for *their* admin costs. The Red Cross then claimed additional costs to fund what they called 'program costs incurred in managing' these third-party projects.

And so the people of Haiti, who were already living in appalling conditions before the earthquake, were now in a worse situation. People live in whatever shelter they can build themselves; there is no running water, and trash and human waste pile up anywhere it can be dumped.

In 2015, 21 staff have either been fired or quit after a variety of scandals; two more are being investigated for alleged sexual misconduct. Plan International, a children's charity, admitted six cases of sex abuse and exploitation against children in July 2016 and June 2017.

It also emerged that Oxfam covered up sex misconduct claims in Haiti. Haiti has suspended Oxfam GB from operating in the country.

> *'Corruption is a cancer that steals from the poor, eats away at governance and moral fiber and destroys trust.'*
>
> *Robert Zoellick*

Don't give up on democracy

As conservativism is challenged and the people who want to hold on to their power base fight for their survival, we find words such as 'liberal' and 'socialist' being bandied around. Politicians use these words as fear tactics to bring us all back into line.

Definition: Liberalism is being willing to respect or accept behaviours or opinions different from one's own; being open to new ideas.

Definition: Socialism refers to any system in which the production and distribution of goods and services *is* a shared responsibility of a group of people. Socialism is based upon economic and political theories that advocate for collectivism. In a state of socialism there is no privately owned property.

What politicians and business leaders are trying to do with the 'socialism' argument is to compare it to communism:

Definition: Communism is a theory or system of social organisation in which all property is owned by the community and each person contributes and receives according to his or her ability and needs. As per the old Soviet Union and Mao Zedong's China where everyone wore a uniform and everyone bent to the will of their illustrious leader.

Communism didn't work but fear of communism absolutely works.

Definition: Social democracy is a political, social and economic philosophy that supports economic and social interventions to promote social justice within the framework of a liberal democratic polity and a capitalist-orientated economy.

Social democracy isn't about ending capitalism; it is about including social services into a capitalist economy. According to the 2019 Democracy Index compiled by *The Economist,* the healthiest and most democratic societies on the planet are proving that society can and must have both:

Norway

Iceland

Sweden

New Zealand

Finland.

These countries work on a framework of social democracy: 'an ideology that has similar values to socialism, but within a capitalist framework. The ideology, named from democracy where people have a say in government actions, supports a competitive economy with money while also helping people whose jobs don't pay a lot.' In other words, entrepreneurialism is encouraged; there are no brakes on getting rich, however, there is also a safety net for the most vulnerable in society.

In Chapter 3, when Philip E. Agre asked and answered 'What is conservatism?', he concluded that 'the true goal of conservatism is to establish an aristocracy, which is a social and psychological condition of inequality. Economic inequality and regressive taxation, while certainly welcomed by the aristocracy, are best understood as a means to their actual goal, which is simply to be aristocrats. It is crucial to conservatism that the people must literally love the order that dominates them.'

The question then becomes, are we currently witnessing a stubborn holding on to 'conservatism', which seems to be the male preference, where the rich get richer and the poor and vulnerable must fend for themselves, or are we seeing a shifting tide where women are saying that's not how we want things to be?

Given that men don't seem inclined to want to change things, then it looks like we women will have to do the job. Even Margaret Thatcher, three times prime minister of Great Britain, was aware of this. She actually declared, 'If you want something said, ask a man; if you want something done, ask a woman.'

> *'When I give food to the poor, they call me a saint. When I ask why the poor have no food, they call me a communist.'*
>
> *Dom Hélder Câmara*

Countries making waves

France became the first nation in the world to ban supermarkets from wasting food under a new law in December 2019. Large grocery stores must now donate unsold food to charities, which will result in millions more meals for France's needy.

The law came on the heels of a grassroots movement by shoppers that aims to expand versions of France's law to all of the European Union. Previously, French supermarkets could trash still-edible food before it even reached its best-before or sell-by dates. Supermarkets will also be banned from intentionally destroying discarded food, notes the *Guardian,* which reports some supermarkets had dumped bleach onto throw-away food to prevent others from eating it.

Check out opportunities to access funding. Canada founded Community Foundations of Canada in 1992 'to support and connect community foundations working across Canada'. More than 90% of Canadian communities have access to funding for community projects. The foundation has combined assets of C$5.8 billion and they put hundreds of millions back into communities.

Environmental initiatives: In Ethiopia volunteers, government officials, and aid workers planted more than 353 million trees. The massive undertaking, if confirmed by outside auditors, shatters the standing world record for the amount of trees planted in a country over the course of 24 hours. The previous world record took place in India when people throughout the country planted 50 million trees in a single day in 2016.

Ethiopia's tree-planting campaign is part of Prime Minister Abiy Ahmed's Green Legacy Initiative, which seeks to revitalise the country's environment and take steps to both mitigate and adapt to climate change. The initiative aims to get four billion trees planted in the years ahead by encouraging each citizen to plant 40 seedlings.

Kenya has a massive challenge finding clean water. One of the country's NGOs set up an initiative called 'Give Power'. Its mission is to install solar technology to help small communities set up desalination systems. These systems transform ocean water into drinking water — previously villagers (mostly women and girls) had to walk up to an hour each day to reach a clean water source.

Farmers across the globe are returning to good old-fashioned environmentally (and bee-friendly) ways of dealing with pest control by planting wild flowers among their crops. Known as the Biological Pest Control Method, the wild flowers negate the need for spraying with deadly toxins, which are decimating not only the bee population but all manner of other insects that form part of the food chain for birds. The added bonus is for the farm workers who no longer have to breathe in and handle toxic chemicals.

And finally, the female president of Chile was determined that when she left office, she would leave behind an environmental legacy. During her term she established five national parks covering 10 million acres. She didn't do this alone. In 2017, Doug Tompkins, founder of the clothing brand The North Face, along with his wife, former CEO of the clothing brand Patagonia, gifted Chile one million acres of land. All parties are committed to leaving a legacy for future generations.

> *'The single biggest threat to our planet is the destruction of habitat and along the way loss of precious wildlife. We need to reach a balance where people, habitat, and wildlife can co-exist — if we don't, everyone loses ... one day.'*
>
> *Steve Irwin*

Questions regarding Chapter 5

What surprised you?

What shocked you?

What made you feel angry?

How have you been affected by the 'shareholder first' policy?

How has your family been affected?

How has your community been affected?

What will you do differently now you know about the unethical companies?

Will you share that knowledge among your friends and networks?

6

YOU CAN MOVE A MOUNTAIN ONE ROCK AT A TIME OR BY CAUSING A GIANT AVALANCHE

'I think you still have no idea the effect you can have.'

Suzanne Collins, Mockingjay

One small person absolutely can make a difference

I'd been speaking at a conference where my topic was 'Dealing with difficult people'. During question time one woman asked how I thought she could deal with a situation in a team of eight women she was part of. Every morning before they started work they would meet in the tea room and have a few minutes chatting. Over the previous few months the 'chats' had turned into trashing the youngest and newest member of the team. Once the young woman arrived everyone would go quiet and start moving to their desks; clearly the poor thing would have been aware of what was going on. Everyone chatting, she walks in the room, everyone disperses. Not a great welcome.

My suggestion was for her to break the chain by making her coffee and then going straight to her desk. She noticed within a few days another woman did the same, then within a week the only person left in the tea room was the person who had clearly started the vendetta: the oldest and least technology-aware person! It wasn't long before this woman decided to retire and the young woman who had been her target blossomed. The tragedy was that if the older team member had been willing to learn about technology, the perfect person to teach her would have been the new young tech-savvy team member.

In such situations, and they are difficult, you can be either part of the problem or part of the solution.

We did discuss some phrases you could use if you felt you needed to speak up. You could say 'This doesn't work' for me or you could say 'This situation is making me feel very uncomfortable.' Be prepared for reactions, of course, but the reactions are the other person's problem, not yours. You have owned your space. It's not unusual once one person has the courage to speak up, others follow.

I do offer a word of caution around 'speaking up'. Don't ever put yourself in danger by doing that. Assess the situation; decide whether it is okay to say 'This isn't working for me' or are you better advised to hold your tongue and work out a better strategy? There are some bosses who do not take kindly to speaking out. Dust off your CV and start looking for your next opportunity. If it is a relative, once again, think carefully the reaction you are likely to get. Will you make the situation better or worse? Is the person likely to listen to you or dismiss you?

Tarana Burke was a small person who made a massive difference. She was working in the area of domestic violence and sexual harassment in the home. Her purpose was to help break women's silence on these issues.

In October 2017, Burke, who at that stage had 500 Twitter followers, picked up the news that Harvey Weinstein had been named by the *New York Times* as a sexual abuser. Burke worked with survivors of sexual abuse and had called her group 'Me Too', at best hoping that the phrase might become a bumper sticker to encourage other victims to seek help. Now suddenly her 'Me Too' slogan has been used over 12 million times because Alyssa Milano, American actress, activist, producer and former singer, had innocently picked up the phrase and turned it into the now-famous #MeToo phrase.

The #MeToo movement gave birth to #TimesUp. This initiative was set up by over 300 women in Hollywood. High-profile leaders like Reese Witherspoon, Natalie Portman and Shonda Rhimes took on the male-based culture of Hollywood, their belief being that every human being deserves the right to earn a living, to take care of their families and to be free of harassment, sexual assault and discrimination.

This in turn led to the Time's Up Legal Defense Fund being launched. Housed and administered by the National Women's Law Center, it will connect any woman who has experienced sexual misconduct with legal and public relations assistance. The fund will help defray costs based on availability of funds; US$21 million was raised in just two months.

These resistance movements led to *Time* magazine naming 'The Silence Breakers' as Person of the Year; they made the women who had stood up and spoken up the stars of 2017.

The other nominees for Person of the Year were no slouches:

Jeff Bezos (Amazon CEO)

The Dreamers (undocumented children of immigrants)

Patty Jenkins (director of *Wonder Woman,* a female-driven box office success story)

Kim Jong-un (North Korean leader)

Colin Kaepernick (NFL player who started the 'kneeling' movement)

The #MeToo movement (women denouncing sexual assault and harassment)

Robert Mueller (Special Counsel investigating Russian collusion)

Mohammed bin Salman (Crown Prince of Saudi Arabia)

Donald Trump (POTUS)

Xi Jinping (President of China).

So in less than a year of Trump becoming POTUS, women who had probably been silent for years about all manner of abuse suddenly decided en masse that 'Enough was enough'. They named and shamed bosses, TV hosts and elected officials for all manner of sexual harassment.

Black American women took down Roy Moore, the Republican

candidate accused of historical sexual misconduct with young girls. Women of all colour went out in force to vote; 98% of black women in Alabama voted for Doug Jones, the Democratic candidate. In his victory speech Doug Jones said: 'This entire race has been about dignity and respect. This campaign has been about the rule of law; about common courtesy and decency and making sure everyone in this state, regardless of which zip code you live in, is going to get a fair shake in life.'

John Carman, the Republican candidate in the November 2017 elections who famously and patronisingly said, 'Will the Women's March protest be over in time for them to cook dinner?' was beaten by a woman.

In November 2017, a letter written by the Alianza Nacional de Campesinas was published in *Time*. It was a letter of solidarity to Hollywood women involved in exposing sexual abuse by Harvey Weinstein. The letter described examples of assault and harassment among roughly 700,000 female farm workers.

Mark Wahlberg donated US$2 million to Time's Up in January 2018 when it was revealed that Wahlberg's co-star in the movie *All the Money in the World*, Michelle Williams, received US$800 for 10 days' work to redo certain scenes in the movie. Wahlberg had received US$1.5 million for the same 10 days of work.

And then I read about two young women who threw all caution to the winds in their quest to save their community.

I'd recently watched the devastating fires that burned millions of hectares of rainforest; most were deliberately lit by people wanting to farm the land and/or mining and logging companies wanting easy access to minerals and thousand-year-old trees. The rainforests are the lungs of the world. They actually clean the toxins from our air and slow down global warming. However, that isn't the only problem; people actually live in the forests. Whole tribes are being moved on or are at risk from the fires.

One such tribe has two brave young women who are taking up the fight to save their forest. Maristela Clediane Uapa Arara is 14 years old and a member of the Arara-Karo indigenous group. She is one of the hunter-gatherer tribes — one of about 900,000 groups that have lived in the rainforest for thousands of years. She is terrified that their land is being taken from them. She and a cousin, 22-year-old Juliana Tuiti Arara, explained: 'It was very sad for us, people from outside are co-opting our indigenous people to log the forest; in the last years, we saw our relatives killing the trees, they came in with bulldozers.' Both girls are determined to hold on to land that their ancestors fought for. When asked how far they would go to fight for their land, both said 'até à morte' (to the death).

> *'I am not free while any woman is unfree, even when her shackles are very different from my own.'*
>
> *Audre Lorde*

Women making waves: the good news

President Obama during his tenure appointed Melanne Verveer to be the first US Ambassador for Global Women's Issues. Verveer believes that 'The denial of women's rights and the oppression of women usually follows "a linear track" to instability.'

To mark 25 years since the United Nations' Fourth World Conference on Women held in Beijing, the 'Women, Peace and Security Index' set forth multiple targets to improve the lives of women around the world. Verveer went on to say: 'We're going to be looking at how much progress we've made in those twenty-five years, and there's been progress, no doubt. Also considerable gaps.'

According to a 2019 National Geographic 'peril, progress and prosperity' study of women in 167 countries, the top 10 countries to be a woman were:

- Norway
- Switzerland
- Finland
- Denmark
- Iceland
- Austria
- UK
- Luxembourg

9=. Sweden/The Netherlands.

New Zealand ranked number 14, the USA 19th and Australia 22nd. So there's still plenty of work to be done.

The five worst countries to be a woman, according to its research, were:

163. South Sudan

164. Pakistan

165. Syria

166. Afghanistan

167. Yemen.

It's easy to think it's all too hard. It is possible to think we are going backwards. It would be easy to settle for what we've already achieved and to think this is as far as we will probably get. Don't give up, because all around the world, various women's groups are determined to help women and girls achieve equality on all fronts, no matter what it takes.

The theme for International Women's Day 2019 was 'Think equal, build smart, innovate for change'. 'Based on current trajectories, existing interventions will not suffice to achieve a Planet 50-50 by 2030. Innovative approaches that disrupt 'business as usual' are central to removing structural barriers and ensuring that no woman and no girl is left behind.' At the end of 2019, 'at a time when the rights of women appear to be being rolled back', they wanted to acknowledge the wins that had been achieved.

- The Solomon Islands: The country's Central Islands Provincial Government endorsed Temporary Special Measures, paving the way for women to take up a quota of leadership positions.

Pacific women: In May, women human rights defenders and feminists from the Pacific convened in Fiji for the second ever Pacific Feminist Forum. They mobilised diverse women from across the Pacific to share knowledge and experiences; to celebrate achievements and create a powerful Pacific Feminist Charter Action Plan.

Young men in Bougainville committed to women's rights: More than 150 men (mostly under the age of 30) from across Bougainville united for a Male Advocates Forum to support the rights of women and children to live free of violence.

Cambodian women raised their voices at the UN. Cambodian women from IWDA's partner organisations advocated 'with tenacity and grit for the rights of women in their country'.

Fijian women campaigned against gender-based violence. A Fiji Women's Freedom Bus took dozens of women and gender-diverse people on a convoy around the main island of Fiji. They facilitated conversations with women on their rights around gender-based violence.

Chilean feminists created a defiant viral anthem: a protest song about rape culture and victim shaming. *Un Violador en Tu Camino*

(A Rapist in Your Path) was first performed in Chile for the International Day for the Elimination of Violence against Women.

The UN published a flagship report, 'Progress of the world's women 2019–2020: Families in a changing world'. The report looked at all manner of economic, demographic, political and social initiatives. The report also looked at the fairness of family laws; employment, unpaid care work, violence against women, and families and migration.

In Ghana, at Makola Market, women traders and vendors are proving that childcare services designed for and managed by the workers themselves have the potential to change their ability to work and earn an income. Expensive childcare had prevented many women from leaving the home, now every morning, 140 children are dropped off at the Makola Market Childcare Centre before their parents start their working day. 'Our aim is that women are able to concentrate on their business and feel good about their children getting a good education from people who care about their wellbeing and their health,' says Aunty Mercy, who is also a trained teacher and manager of the centre.

After years of relentless campaigning, northern Africa and western Asia finally removed archaic laws that had for decades forced women to marry their rapists. In the space of a month, the governments of Tunisia, Jordan and finally Lebanon repealed or reformed clauses in their penal codes that enabled perpetrators to evade prosecution if they married the woman they had attacked. The law also allowed families not to force women into marriage with their rapists to prevent the social stigma of premarital sex.

> *'The beauty of measures and indexes is that people look at them — men in particular! Men really do want to know if they are 'winning' and where they 'rank'. So if that's what men want and need, and if measures and indexes are the things to bring women*

out of subjugation, if a checklist and a 'ranking' saves the planet, then keep measuring!'

Ann Andrews

Finding your voice: finding your tribe

As you've read the stories of all manner of courageous women so far, who excited you? Who scared you? Who inspired you? Who would you like to be like?

Women are so good at playing small, fearing that they can do nothing to change anything. I once interviewed a female doctor in my early days of running women's workshops, and she said several times 'I'm just a general practitioner'! Notice how many times you say 'just'. The word minimises what comes next. When I'm working with female groups I ask them various questions:

What did you want to be when you were a little girl?

Did your parents encourage you to follow that dream?

Did your teachers encourage you?

At what point did you give up on the dream?

When do you think you might revisit that dream?

What's holding you back from making a start?

What roadblocks do you put in your way?

What would you do if money/children/partners/time weren't obstacles?

What would you do if you knew you couldn't fail?

If you won Lotto, what would you do differently?

What do you regret?

What are you teaching your daughters/nieces?

What are your current goals?

What books do you read?

What TV programmes do you watch?

Who inspires you?

Who would you like to help?

What gives you a sense of satisfaction?

Often women will say they have no time; and I understand that. Busy mums, most who work; some who even have two jobs. Every day can be a blur of rushing from one task to the next. To these women I say make a donation of money to some charity you believe in. It doesn't have to be a large amount of money; the price of a coffee once per month to a charity will make a difference. If 100 people donate \$5, that's \$500; if 1000 people donate \$5, that's \$5000. That's a whole lot of services a charity can offer for the cost of a coffee.

However, choose your charity wisely; you've just seen the Red Cross and Oxfam are pretty suspect. Before you donate your hard-earned money to anyone, check them out, in particular, check how much of your donation goes to admin costs and how much actually reaches the people it needs to reach. To the women who say they have no money, I suggest give some time. Half a day at the SPCA once per month will help them immensely; a couple of hours once per week to sit with a lonely pensioner will change his or her world.

> *'Generosity is giving more than you can, and pride is taking less than you need.'*
>
> *Kahlil Gibran*

Heading into a world where values are valued

If we revisit the 'virtues' on which 'The Inn of the Eight Happinesses' was based, they were actually eight values: love, virtue, gentleness, tolerance, loyalty, truth, beauty and devotion.

Values definition: The regard that something is held to deserve; the importance, worth, or usefulness of something; principles or standards of behaviour; one's judgment of what is important in life.

My 30+ years of working with organisations have been based around helping particular owners or managers to work out what their business or team stands for. Initially their reaction will invariably be 'to make a profit'. Yes, of course making a profit is important; you wouldn't be in business for very long if you didn't make a profit. The problem comes when making a profit is all that matters.

When I encourage business owners to dig down and consider 'how' they make a profit, a whole different set of answers emerges. That's when they may add the importance of great customer service; the need for delivering a quality product or service; their determination to ensure delivery times and realistic return policies. Once they start using words like that, they are actually starting to define their 'values'.

Values are simply what's important to us, whether that is a team, a company, an individual or a family. Values are the way we do things around here. When a company is clear on its values, when it recruits and promotes to its values, amazing things happen because everyone knows what's important. When businesses are not clear on their values, when they recruit to whatever the mood of the day is and when they promote people for all the wrong reasons, that's when all manner of challenges arise.

As individuals we need to be very clear what our own values are.

Our heroes, the ones who gave up careers to care for someone, put their values before their income. Our warriors do likewise. Lucy Lawless would not have climbed a 53-metre drilling derrick mast if she wasn't passionate about the environment; she put that value before the value of her own personal safety even while admitting that she was terrified.

There's a wonderful team-building exercise where a team member is offered a thousand dollars to cross a massive raging river on a very, very fragile rope bridge; most people decline. Even when the offer is raised to a million dollars, very few people opt for the money. However, if we say 'your youngest child has been trapped on the other side of the bridge', not a single parent in the team would hesitate. That's how values work.

Ellen DeGeneres said: 'I stand for honesty, equality, kindness, compassion, treating people the way you want to be treated, and helping those in need. To me, those are traditional values.' Currently we have a world where so many values are being tested, if not trashed. The environment is being put at risk, the rich are getting richer and working families are struggling to stay afloat.

Our global values need to be addressed. And soon.

> *'I will not let oil companies write the country's energy plan or endanger our coastlines or collect another four billion dollars in corporate welfare from our taxpayers.'*
>
> *President Obama*

What would kindness do?

I was speaking to a Rotary club on the topic of leadership and was comparing leaders who put the economy before their people. Rotarians all over the world are known for their charitable works, so I was stunned when one member of the audience took exception to what I was saying. He called out, 'So you're not happy that New Zealand has this rock star economy?' I replied, 'I'm delighted that we have a rock star economy. My sadness comes from the fact that while we are being lauded across the globe for our economy, we are in the middle of one of the coldest and wettest winters in years, and we have a record number of families sleeping in cars. I would rather have a little bit less "rock" and a little bit more "compassion".'

This man's reaction got me thinking. How could this person be willing to belong to an organisation that is based on good work yet be so antagonistic at the thought of a government doing the same? Back to the socialism versus capitalism argument. Surely we can do both?

We've just seen that Norway, Finland, etc. are ranked the best in the world and are social democracies; capitalism is encouraged but the most vulnerable in their societies are looked after. I'm not sure why anyone could find that idea repugnant or offensive or threatening.

On further reflection though, I wondered if those charitable acts were an extension of 'paternalism', the thought being that our helping out people less fortunate than ourselves gives people a sense of 'goodness'. There's nothing wrong with doing charitable acts, but what if people became sufficiently able to look after themselves that they didn't need charity? Wouldn't that be a great society? Does keeping people poor actually offer an opportunity for the givers of charity to feel a bit superior, and even just a little bit smug?

Fortunately, there are many, many movements that are similarly tired of money being the be-all and end-all of our world.

If you are familiar with the phrase 'pay it forward', you may be surprised to learn that the concept of paying it forward actually dates back to 317 BC and was a play performed in ancient Athens.

Many people are, by their very nature, generous. Benjamin Franklin famously said, 'When I'm employed in serving others, I do not look upon myself as conferring favours but in paying debts.'

Mostly, the pay-it-forward theme is about money. I heard of one young mum who got to the checkout and didn't have enough money to buy her groceries; the person behind her paid the difference.

The *Pay It Forward* novel by Catherine Ryan Hyde was turned into a movie starring Kevin Spacey and Helen Hunt. Their obligation was to do three good deeds for others after someone had done one good deed for them, the idea being that a threefold kindness would spread exponentially unleashing a social movement that would make the world a better place.

A social movement did spin off after the movie. Pay It Forward Day has become a worldwide celebration of kindness celebrated annually on 28 April. The day encourages people to #standforkindness and to inspire acts of generosity, not just on the day itself but continuing for the entire year.

Xero Australia recently took up the challenge by asking every office in Australia to nominate a business they wanted to pay it forward to. Xero sent out people to call on these business — cafes, barbers and gyms — in advance of the initiative. When customers went to pay for their services, they were given a card which said 'This one has been paid for you by Xero.'

Anne Herbert started a 'Random Acts of Kindness' movement in a Sausalito, California café. She simply wrote 'Practice random acts of kindness and senseless acts of beauty' on one of their placemats, and a whole movement was born.

Many countries now have a 'Random Acts of Kindness Day'. If you check out the 'Random Acts of Kindness' website, you will find ideas for acts of kindness in the workplace and in schools, not to mention all manner of resources you can utilise.

And if you think business and generosity doesn't pay off — understand the 'Archie Effect'.

In 2019, the infant son of Prince Harry and Meghan Markle was pictured in Canada wearing a grey beanie. The picture went viral and it seemed that every mother of a small child wanted an 'Archie' hat. On further investigation into the business that made the hat, we find a New Zealand community enterprise called Make Give Love. The co-founder of the business said that during the couple's recent tour of Australia and New Zealand, they sent the hat as a gift never expecting it to feature in a photo. Orders went ballistic. From selling around 45 hats per month to selling around 300 a day!

What's happening behind the scenes of the hat is a whole lot of women gathering together once a week to knit or crochet a hat for a mental health cause. The groups meet in a café, have a group leader and then sit and knit. The company provides the materials and people knit for free. The generosity doesn't stop there — for every hat that is purchased, one is given away to someone in need, either a homeless person, a deprived child, a refugee or a rough sleeper. So simple, so kind, so generous. The added bonus is for the knitters; they now are part of a group that meets and chats once a week, helping them also. A whole generation of grandmothers learned to knit and were possibly sitting at home alone and lonely. Now they can be part of one of the groups.

The words 'generosity' and 'kindness' are not necessarily words you associate with business. Yet Dame Anita Roddick all those years ago decided that her employees would spend one day a month in the community doing something for someone else. That is generosity, that is kindness.

Kindness at work could take so many forms. Factoring in the need for working mums to leave dead on 5 p.m. is a kindness. Great bosses treat their people as human beings. Great bosses will know if one of their team is going through a relationship break-up; or that someone has just had a miscarriage. Stuff happens to all of us at some time, which means that as employees we may not be on the top of our game for a while. Great bosses make allowances for us.

Treat people well and they will give back tenfold.

> *'Three things in human life are important: the first is to be kind; the second is to be kind; and the third is to be kind.'*
>
> *Henry James*

Icelandic women lighting the way

In late 2008, during the global financial crisis, all three of Iceland's privately owned banks collapsed. This in turn led to a severe economic depression for the next two years and generated considerable political unrest.

All three banks had grown rapidly driven by access to cheap and easy credit in the international banking market. As early warning signs of a global financial crisis started to emerge, international investors in Iceland became nervous and so the rapid withdrawal of money from the country began. No bank can sustain rapid funds withdrawal and so it was only a matter of time before an economic downward spiral began for Iceland.

Investors pulled out, the krona was devalued and problems for Icelandic banks to do business became even more difficult. In 2007, Iceland's external debt was seven times its GDP; by 2008, it had become 11 times its GDP.

Trust in banks in Iceland hit an all-time low. The government instituted an emergency law that allowed the Financial

Supervisory Authority to completely take over the banking system. The old banks were put into receivership resulting in massive losses for shareholders and foreign creditors.

History will show that Iceland's bankers were overwhelmingly male and had become reckless and out of control. Women now head up all Iceland's banks. The crisis also led to the collapse of the government — Jóhanna Sigurðardóttir was Iceland's premier, the world's first openly gay leader (stepped down in 2013).

The banking crisis turned into a massive opportunity for women to step into positions vacated by the very men who were now blamed for the crisis. The stated intention of all these women was to create a more balanced economy by instilling values that are traditionally female: openness, fairness and social responsibility!

Ruth Sunderland wrote an article, 'After the crash, Iceland's women lead the rescue'. She travelled to Reykjavik to interview the women now running the country. She heard how 'they are determined to reinvent business and society by injecting values of openness, fairness and social responsibility'.

Three Icelandic women have joined forces to spread those values. Halla Tómasdóttir, Kristin Petursdóttir and the singer Björk set up an investment fund to boost the decimated economy by investing in green technology. Petursdóttir, a former senior banking executive, and Tómasdóttir, the former managing director of the Iceland Chamber of Commerce, had already set up a firm teaching female values in the mainly male spheres of private equity, wealth management and corporate advice.

These values are:

Risk awareness. We will not invest in things we don't understand.

Profit with principles. Not just economic profit, but a positive social and environmental impact.

Emotional capital. When we invest, we do an emotional due diligence — or check — on the company. We look at the people, at whether the corporate culture is an asset or a liability.

Straight talking. We believe the language of finance should be accessible, and not part of the alienating nature of banking culture.

Independence. We would like to see women increasingly financially independent, because with that comes the greatest freedom to be who you want to be, and also unbiased advice.

The final outcome for the male bankers in the Icelandic meltdown was that 36 bankers ended up with 96 years in jail. Eleven of the bankers were sentenced to a total of 35 years in prison; another seven were sentenced to a total of 25 years, and former employees of Landsbankinn received 13 years in total.

Despite a global financial crash and despite Icelandic banks being taken over by their government and despite 36 bankers ending up in jail, Australian bankers just kept merrily along fleecing their customers.

It would appear that since 2013, Australian banks have been turning a blind eye to 'frequent low-value payments to the Philippines', a sign of the purchase of live-streaming child exploitation material.

A Royal Commission was set up after rumblings and suspicions of all manner of other questionable practices.

The banks had been accused of making people homeless; of turning yet another blind eye to clear indications of people with gambling problems, for charging fees for non-existent services and even charging dead customers.

Rough estimates are that the four big Australian banks fleeced customers out of A$178 million for service they didn't even provide. Compensation costs will be in the region of A$850 million.

How could that have happened? How could anyone in the senior echelons of those four banks think that what they were doing was okay? Did they honestly think they would never be found out? Is there a kind of blindness that occurs around people who set up scams and continue them regardless of the pain? It must surely take a particular kind of arrogance to fleece people who are already in dire straits financially.

Perhaps some of the Icelandic female bankers could be seconded to show Australian bankers how to become ethical again.

Hopefully, as per the Icelandic reaction, criminal charges will follow.

> *'Our Björk fund is to focus on sustainable growth. Iceland was the first in the world into the crisis, but we could be the first out, and women have a big role to play in that. It goes back to our Viking women. While the men were out there raping and pillaging, the women were running the show at home.'*
>
> *Halla Tómasdóttir*

Questions regarding Chapter 6

What surprised you?

What depressed you?

Which story impacted the most for you?

What inspired you?

Did you go through the questions in Chapter 4?

How did you fare in answering them?

Have you worked out your value system?

Do you already have a 'tribe' or a group you belong to?

Would you like to belong to a group?

Could you start a group?

Who do you know that you could invite?

7

HAVE YOU FULFILLED YOUR DESTINY? IF NOT, WHY NOT?

'I want to be thoroughly used up when I die, for the harder I work, the more I live. Life is no 'brief candle' to me. It is a sort of splendid torch which I have got hold of for a moment, and I want to make it burn as brightly as possible before handing it on to the future generations.'

George Bernard Shaw

Welcome to your destiny

We've looked at all manner of people and challenges in this book. Now I want to focus on you, the reader. I became aware of the word 'woke' recently and wanted to know what the word meant.

Definition: 'Woke is a political term which refers to an awareness of issues concerning social and racial justice. It is derived from the African-American expression 'stay woke', meaning be aware of the issues. In African American vernacular it means 'being aware of the truth behind things "the man" doesn't want you to know, i.e. classism, racism, and any other social injustices'.

So many of the problems we witness on a daily basis seem way bigger than anything we can tackle as individuals. Dame Anita Roddick once said, 'If you think you're too small to make a difference, try going to bed with a mosquito in the room.'

Over the school holidays, we had two grandchildren staying. Our grandchildren are all heading into their teen years now, so keeping them occupied is a whole lot more challenging than when they were toddlers. One wet and miserable afternoon we got to talking about jobs, which led to talking about careers, which led to talking about a person's 'destiny', a concept that was new to both of them.

I dug out my very battered numerology book, *The Future Seekers,* by Kimberley Patterson, and we looked at their birth dates and calculated what numerology suggests is a life path for each of them. They were utterly fascinated and hopefully they will aim a little higher than 'job' after our afternoon together.

If you are curious as to *your* destiny and where you can make a difference, this is how you do it:

Write down your full date of birth, e.g. 3.4.1956, then add them together: 3 + 4+ 1 + 9 + 5 + 6 = 28. Now add these two numbers together: 2 + 8 = 10. Break this last number down to a single digit: 1 + 0 = 1.

The purpose of breaking everything down into a single digit is to be able to work out your actual life path. There are nine years in a 'destiny' cycle, and this person is a number 1. There are three double numbers you do *not* break down into a single number, but more on that later.

Ones are our pioneers and independent spirits. One is described at the vibration of the King Maker. These people make their own way in life and success depends on their own talents and abilities. They can be highly inspirational and creative. There is, however, a need to avoid an overly strong focus on 'self'. Famous 1s: Florence Nightingale, Audre Lorde, Ayn Rand, Maya Angelou, Lady Gaga, Megyn Kelly, Amy Klobuchar, Janis Joplin.

Twos are born in the vibration of co-operation, diplomacy and sensitivity. These people like to follow the lead of others, are very affectionate, can be idealistic and are warm and loving. There is a need to be discerning about the motives of those you admire. Famous 2s: Gladys Aylward, Rosa Parks.

Three is the number of self-expression, or artistic ability, the joy of performing and operating in social circumstances. Their challenge is to find a defined path in all of their interests otherwise they can spend their lives scattered. Famous 3s: Katy Perry, Rihanna, Queen Victoria, Kate Middleton, Hillary Clinton, Margaret Sanger.

Fours are practical hard workers, they are self-disciplined, precise and down to earth. These people are responsible but need to guard against stubbornness. Famous 4s: the Dalai Lama, Madeleine Albright, Meghan Markle, Barbara Bush, Zainab Salbi, Dolly Parton, Celeste Barber (the comedienne who started a massive fundraiser for Australian bush fires).

Oprah, one of my warriors, is a 4.

Fives are restless, busy people with strong skills in communication. They are highly changeable and there is a strong need to control the thoughts. This is a number that speaks of a love of travel and an enthusiasm for life. The lesson of 5s is the constructive use of freedom. There is a need to focus and not scatter and waste their energies. Famous 5s: Helen Keller, Theresa May, Ellen DeGeneres, Alyssa Milano, Marianne Williamson, Tina Turner, Tarana Burke, Sanna Marin (recently became the youngest prime minister in the world at just 34 years old).

Four of my warriors are 5s: Alexandria Ocasio-Cortez, J.K. Rowling, and Kamala Harris. Emma González's birthdate is 11.11.1999; watch out for this young woman.

Sixes are about expressing love for others. This is also a responsible number, often the number of those who guide others. There is a strong sense of harmony in their lives along with creative abilities. There is a need to be kinder to themselves. Famous 6s: Saint Joan of Arc, Eleanor Roosevelt, Dame Jane Goodall (one of my warriors).

Sevens have an energy of mysticism. These people are highly sensitive, have an affinity with things psychic and often choose careers to do with religion or spirituality. The ability to help others understand the esoteric realms is also indicated. These people may have difficulty in being understood by others. Famous 7s: Princess Diana, Queen Elizabeth, Taylor Swift, Susan Sarandon, Farrah Fawcett, Marilyn Monroe, Golda Meir.

Five of my warriors are 7s: Nancy Pelosi, Ruth Bader Ginsburg, Angela Merkel, Bette Midler, and Melinda Gates.

Eights can master big business, finance and material dealings. These people are practical and grounded. There may be many obstacles to overcome but success is offered if challenges are met.

There is an inherent spiritual ability that can be tapped into. There is a need to guard against making money and power the total focus in life. Famous 8s: Emmeline Pankhurst, Beyoncé, Aung San Suu Kyi, Amy Winehouse, Isabel Allende.

Jane Fonda is an 8.

Nines are completing many lifetimes of work. These people are the humanitarians, they are selfless and deeply caring. The lesson for 9s is in finding love and satisfaction: their challenge is not to lose themselves by almost giving up the idea of needing personal satisfaction. Famous 9s: Mother Teresa, Edith Cavell, Gloria Steinem, Louisa May Alcott, Bette Davis, Cher, Serena Williams, Winnie Mandela.

Four of my warriors are 9s: Louise Hay, Greta Thunberg, Malala Yousafzai and Marie Yovanovitch.

Winnie Mandela is a 9. That is a humanitarian number. She sits alongside four of my warriors: Louise Hay, Greta Thunberg, Malala Yousafzai and Marie Yovanovitch. She was married to one of the century's most beloved leaders, Nelson Mandela. He chose the high road even after being imprisoned for years; sadly, it appears she chose the low road.

Which brings us to the three numbers you do *not* break down to one digit.

If your birth numbers add up to 11 or 22 or the incredibly rare 33, then you are truly gifted and you are absolutely on a path of vital importance. People with these master numbers will have a heightened sense of intuition, potential and intelligence.

For example, if a person's birth date was 4.4.1956, that would look like: 4 + 4 + 1 + 9 + 5 + 6 = 29, and 2 + 9 = 11.

Master number 11 — The Old Soul

Master number 11 is considered to be the most intuitive of all the master numbers as it represents intuition, insight, a connection to your subconscious and your gut feelings. Those who possess the master number 11 in their date or birth charts are thought to be old souls and able to deal with stressful situations in a calm and relaxed manner.

This number is associated with faith and those who can predict the future, such as psychics, clairvoyants and prophets. Those who have the master number 11 tend to be respectful, show empathy and an understanding of others with an ability to put themselves in someone else's shoes.

One negative attribute of this number is that if the person has not concentrated their efforts on a specific goal, then they are in danger of experiencing intense fear and anxiety, which could lead to phobias and panic attacks.

Elevens are highly sensitive and idealistic. These people have special skills in inspiring others, possibly even in foreseeing the future. They can rise to the top of their field. There is, however, a strong need to ground dreams in the real world and to carry through their grand ideals into practical expression. They need to guard against becoming dreamers rather than doers. Famous women with a master number 11: Jacqueline Kennedy, Madonna, Gwen Stefani, Tina Tchen (#TimesUp).

Two of my warriors fall into this category: Michelle Obama and Lucy Lawless. President Obama is also an 11; no wonder he and Michelle are such a power couple.

Master number 22 — The Master Builder

This birth number has the power to turn dreams into reality. The number 22 contains all the intuition and insights of the master number 11 but with added practicality and a disciplined manner.

They have big plans, great ideas and huge potential; add this to leadership skills and high self-esteem and you have the making of great personal success. Twenty-two is associated with great thinkers, those with huge confidence and those who always live up to their potential. Those who have 22 in their charts tend to be able to make dreams come to life, turning their goals into fruition in a very rapid way. Negative traits include a lack of practical ability which does not allow them to realise their huge potential.

Twenty-twos live and encourage the highest ideals of mankind. This is an incredibly rare number. This person would be a modern-day King Arthur. It speaks of many lives in preparation of this incarnation, coupled with an inherent ability to be a master of life. Life will bring many challenges and tests. The key here is to learn balance. These people will work for humanity. Twenty-twos have huge potential if the power they are given is properly handled. Other famous people with a master number 22 are Margaret Thatcher and Nikki Haley. Dame Anita Roddick, one of my warriors, was a 22.

NB: Marie Antoinette was a 22, she who said 'Let them eat cake'. Just because we are born with one of these high numbers doesn't necessarily mean we will use our talents for the good of mankind; we are born with choice so we can just as easily work against humanity as for the good of it.

Margaret Thatcher is a prime example of this: to her followers she was a hero, to the working class of the UK she was a monster.

Master number 33 — The Master Teacher

Arguably the most influential of all numbers is the 33. It is the most powerful because the number 33 also contains the 11 and the 22 and, therefore, upgrades these two other numbers to the top level.

Master number 33 has no personal ambition, instead, they want to bring about a spiritual uplifting of all mankind. Thirty-three is associated with complete devotion, rare wisdom and understanding without communication. A typical 33 will concentrate on humanitarian issues and give themselves entirely to a project. Those who have 33 in their charts will be extremely knowledgeable but also very emotional. Negative traits include an emotional imbalance and a tendency to flare up on emotional issues.

Famous women with a master number 33: Salma Hayek, Margaret Atwood (*The Handmaid's Tale*), Taslima Nasrin (Bangladeshi-Swedish writer, physician, feminist, human rights activist, known for her writing on women's oppression and her outspoken criticism of religion).

Numerology experts believe that when you put all the master numbers together, they represent a triangle of enlightenment:

Master number 11 represents vision.

Master number 22 combines this vision with action.

Master number 33 offers guidance to the world.

Two of my warriors have the number 33: Linda Ronstadt and Elizabeth Warren, and we currently have two female country leaders with the number 33: Tsai Ing-wen, President of Taiwan; and Jacinda Ardern, Prime Minister of New Zealand.

Because a 33 birth number is so rare, I wondered which famous men might fall into this powerful category. I found Stephen King, Robert De Niro, Albert Einstein, John Lennon, Francis Ford Coppola and Thomas Edison.

> *'Pick your battles,' she muttered in her ear. 'I am! I'm picking this one!'*
>
> *Lauren James, Another Beginning*

Questions regarding Chapter 7

What is your 'woke' from this chapter?

What concerns you socially, environmentally?

What irritates you?

What gets under your skin?

What seems unfair to you?

What would you change if you could?

What is your destiny number?

What do you think you could be here to do?

Are you fulfilling your destiny?

If not, what is holding you back?

What roadblocks/excuses are you putting in your own way?

Are you playing small?

When will you start believing in yourself?

What will you do to make *your* mark going forward?

8

IF NOT ME, THEN WHO? IF NOT NOW, THEN WHEN?

'There is a vitality, a life force, a quickening that is translated through you into action, and because there is only one of you in all time, this expression is unique. And if you block it, it will never exist through any other medium and will be lost.'

Martha Graham

You're never too old and it's never too late

After our grandchildren went back home and after I'd done the 'destiny' exercise with them, I was left feeling very out of sorts. I'd had over 30 years of a very successful career speaking at conferences on all manner of HR topics. Inevitably people would stay behind after my sessions and ask me to help them with in-house issues. I earned a very nice living; I got to travel all over New Zealand, occasionally to Australia, and had even spoken at conferences in Hong Kong, Singapore and Belgium.

And then I wrote the first book about Donald Trump.

Almost overnight my phone stopped ringing; four conferences were cancelled and my income vanished. I was stunned. I was writing about an appalling leader; a liar and a bully, and no-one wanted to know. Left with no work and no income, I wrote the second book about *Leaders Behaving Badly*, a follow-on from the Trump book, but also a book about people who were standing up to him and leaders like him. Not a lot changed; I did find a bit of work with a couple of my older clients, but I had certainly hit a brick wall both work-wise and financially.

I pondered my age; I was no longer a spring chicken. Perhaps potential clients were viewing me as old and possibly past it. I began the usual self-talk of 'time to slow down', 'time to accept the fact that you are over the hill'. And then I did the destiny exercise with our grandchildren. You see, I'm an 11. One of those master numbers. I've always felt I was here to do something powerful. I thought for years that nursing people was my 'calling' — that didn't work out, so clearly that was not my destiny.

After joining the Women's Royal Navy I had a ball; I had no regrets about the change of career. I chugged along, got married, had my children, started a speaking career, set up my own business. Life was good. However, for several years I had been feeling unsettled and I had no idea why. I put it down to age; I blamed the economy; I kept doing everything I'd always done, but brick walls seemed to be everywhere.

Being reminded of my 11 was actually a giant wake-up call.

I started having what I describe as 'funny little dreams'. I've had them all my life, mostly the ordinary clearing-type dreams that everyone has, but every now and again I would have a dream that would literally wake me up, and strangely enough when having one of these funny little dreams, I always seem to wake at 3.33 or 4.44.

Within a couple of weeks of our grandchildren leaving I had the first of several dreams. The first was a dream where I was actually watching myself trying to hack my way through a really thick hedge with very blunt shears. I'm part of a woman's group and I jokingly told them about my dream and of course, as women do, one of my female friends asked me what I thought the dream was about. I confessed I wasn't sure, but thought it was probably to do with this unsettled feeling I'd been having — basically trying to go forward when nothing seemed to be working out. Mmmm.

In my second dream a few days later, I was driving my car the wrong way down a road. Interpretation, I was going the wrong way in my life? And my third dream literally the very next night found me in my car yet again, driving down the wrong road, only this time I got out of the car, looked around and over to my left I saw the road I needed to be on.

I'd been working with mostly male leaders for all of my life. My unsettledness was actually my frustration that they just weren't 'getting' what I was trying to teach them. In my humble opinion, they too were on the wrong road; this endless quest for profits. I was frustrated when their solution to everything was cut costs by laying people off and the savings in wages and salaries would make the bottom line healthier. For now!

Very few companies really live their values; they espouse them, they put them on a brass plaque on the wall in reception, but when push comes to shove and they've had a bad quarter, it becomes sell all the rubbish you can because we need to make our quarterly results look good. And I was getting increasingly disheartened with this thinking.

So reminding myself that I am an 11, admittedly a very old 11; having the conversation with my lovely neighbour about Gladys Aylward and her heroism; watching all the amazing women right now who are saying 'Enough!', feeling in my bones that what is happening isn't right, that we've lost the plot, is what got me right here, writing this book about women and for women.

If you've been reading this book thinking you are too old to pick up on any of the challenges I've put in front of you, please think again.

In the UK, USA and EU alone, 6.5 million over 50s are unemployed. According to The Age and Employment Network, 'If you become unemployed in your 50s and remain unemployed for more than a year, you are more likely to die or start drawing your pension than ever get a job again.' How depressing is that? What a tragic waste of talent, knowledge and experience.

As humans we are designed to live for 120 years, so 45 isn't even halfway through our life span. I know some 70-year-olds who have more passion and energy than many 18-year-olds. Yet companies tend to recruit the 18-year-olds over older workers, even knowing that young people have no life experience and may even arrive with that 'you owe me' attitude so many young people seem to have these days.

I'd like to start a revolution around rethinking 'age'. Organisations need to re-evaluate their negativity to older workers and factor in all their wonderful experience. Can an 18-year-old manage a team or a project? Can you send them out to chat to angry customers? Can you safely trust them to manage a budget yet? And do we really want a society where all these amazing older people are languishing on benefits at the most productive times of their lives?

It staggers me to find how few people set goals. We spend more time planning a holiday than we spend thinking about our career. Sadly, a lot of older workers quietly slip into what I call 'quit and stay' mode — the body shows up each day to do their job but the heart, soul and passion are elsewhere. Sooner or later that kind of thinking takes a toll: it takes a toll on their health and it takes a toll on their boss's perception of them as being 'dead wood'. So to the 45/50-year-olds, male and female, reading this, here are my thoughts:

- Volunteer for anything and everything.
- Develop a 'pick me' attitude.
- Be totally on top of technology.
- Get those five-year goals sorted and work towards them every day of your life.
- Work out what your real passion in life is and if need be, turn that into your very own business because if you own your own business, no-one (except your bank manager) can ever make you redundant again.
- Buy a franchise with your redundancy money. It may not be your long-term desire but you will be taught how to run a business and given the coaching and mentoring required to make your business successful. *Then* you will be ready to start your own business.
- Start a gathering of like-minded people who want to tackle an issue no matter how small.

If ever there was a group or tribe that could pick up the reins of some of the social issues we are facing and make a difference, it is this group. We are older and more mature. We've seen and survived all manner of crises, we are a group that can absolutely start a revolution.

If you are 50+ and have just been made redundant, dust off your CV for sure; apply for jobs absolutely, but as you wait for the phone to ring asking you to come and be interviewed, fill your spare time with thinking about the things that annoy you or concern you. Ask a few people to join you for a coffee and see if whatever is concerning you concerns them. See if you can start your own small group of change makers.

Don't ever give up hope. Believe in yourself and others will believe in you, because you really are never too old and it really is never too late.

Work out your destiny number; take notice of your gut feelings; make notes about your dreams. Who knows which road you could find yourself taking.

> *'I long to accomplish great and noble tasks, but it is my chief duty to accomplish humble tasks as though they were great and noble. The world is moved along, not only by the mighty shoves of its heroes, but also by the aggregate of the tiny pushes of each honest worker.'*
>
> *Helen Keller*

The kitchen table warriors

This story is an extract from a chapter I wrote for a joint–venture book a few years ago. Fifty authors were asked to imagine what society would look like 50 years hence. It is a fictional story, but very relevant to the things I've talked about so far and hopefully the story will give readers an idea on how to get started with whatever they would like to change.

> I'd been working as a teacher aid when in 2016 several events created a terrifying political storm. Continuous war in the Middle East unleashed an array of terror setting off a tidal wave of humanity fleeing to safety. Britain was knee deep in leaving the European Union. The EU had been built on the ideal of open borders, which had caused millions of people to migrate to

countries promising a better way of life. Whole countries seemed to be emptying while others filled to overflowing.

An ever-shrinking employment market caused by advances in technology led to distressing reverberations for families and communities. Western middle classes suddenly found themselves unemployed, poor and angry. Globalisation had failed. The promised 'trickle down' effect hadn't eventuated, in fact the reverse happened: the rich kept getting richer, leaving the poor further and further behind.

And finally, a divisive man tapped into the underbelly of American discontent and became President of the USA. He promised to bring back jobs. His slogan 'Make America Great Again' was really a smoke screen to 'Make America White Again'.

These combined events created a global chain reaction of nationalism, fear, protest and unrest.

I'd studied Alvin Toffler's book *The Third Wave* at teacher training college. Toffler identified three periods of massive societal disruption. An Agricultural Age morphed into an Industrial Age, which in turn became the The Age of Technology. As society passed from one age to the next, traditional jobs vanished. Wage earners would be caught unprepared and untrained for the new opportunities that were created. Given time, of course, the changes simply became the new way we did things and people adapted. In 2016, I watched the world crash headlong into a Fourth Wave.

In America we were horrified as our new president verbally abused immigrants, marginalised women and vilified gays, lesbians and transgenders. I was in the thick of my first ever march the day after his election. As he continued to pour out verbal abuse, I gathered together similarly disgruntled colleagues and we hit social media with our fears and concerns.

Initially our gatherings were just about people venting. And that was okay. It felt like something we all needed to do. One day a strange question was asked: 'I wonder who will stand up to him?' Which led to more of us asking 'I wonder what "they" will do about the immigrants/healthcare situation/poor wages/loss of jobs, etc.

etc. etc.' The mysterious 'they' we all talk about when something isn't working the way we would like it to.

And so we became 'they'. Because so many of our conversations had begun with the words 'I wonder', we decided to call ourselves 'Wonder Women', and so began the move from being a group of women bitching at a kitchen table about things we felt powerless to understand or fix, to becoming the Wonder Women who started to fix things.

Inch by inch, day by day, our small discontented groups rapidly mutated into powerful lobby groups.

Our parents thought our dissent would be a five-day wonder, but what happened was to change the face of society. Not by governments or elected officials (the mysterious 'they'), but by ordinary people and mostly by us, the millennials. For the first time ever, we mobilised and marched. We fought for our future.

It's now 50 years since those events.

People passionate about education influenced schools, saying, 'We have to stop teaching kids to look for jobs, we need our kids to be taught life skills so if they are made redundant they don't fall into depression and loss of self-worth.'

Some lobbied for change in the welfare system. Their belief was that the money spent on people without jobs should be put into training these people so they could find another job. Paying people to sit on a sofa all day not only cost the taxpayer but it created a vicious cycle of low self-esteem and apathy. They wanted wellbeing centres set up; places where people could upskill and retrain.

Other groups took on the health sector; some championed the 'green' movement, taking on the fossil fuel giants, the plastics sector and anyone else that caused damage to an increasingly fragile ecology.

No sector was safe! A movement was born. We marched, protested and lobbied. We joined forces with other movements. We took on anyone and everyone who stood in our way. We claimed back our future from any government official stuck in obsolete thinking and vested in self-interest.

Millennials across the world chorused 'Enough!' We no longer live in a world of white and we will not sit around while apathetic governments do nothing. We shouted collectively and clearly that we now lived in a multicultural, multi-gender, borderless world and women and minorities would not be silenced. We made it abundantly clear that the future had to be about people and planet before profits and that any organisation that put profits before people would be named and shamed. And we also made it clear that any government officials who stood in our way would be lobbied against and voted out.

As Wonder Women we asked tough questions:

'Just because robots can work 24/7 to churn out "stuff", does that mean they should?'

'Just because we can keep drilling for oil and gas at huge cost to the environment, does that mean we should?'

'Just because we can run our businesses without any human help at all, does that mean we should?'

Every initiative we heard touted by corporates or governments, we took to social media and asked:

Who will this benefit?

Who or what will this hurt?

We were clear that people and the environment had to be top priority; if either was hurt we named and shamed, publicly and vehemently. Corporates got the message really quickly as their sales and reputations crashed overnight.

Within 15 years we'd changed the education system. Teachers now taught kids how to learn and adapt; to understand that 'jobs' were virtually obsolete. They stressed that work was more likely to be short-term projects; that work could be transient and even done online and from home. Kids are told that's the new reality. Get over it.

One community trialled a universal wage. Initially one level of payment to everyone, but eventually, at our insistence, two levels of payment were implemented. A basic living wage for people who couldn't contribute to society for whatever reason, and a larger amount for people who were willing to give back or help out in some way.

Older workers often became coaches/mentors or trainers. Younger and fitter people chose to help as volunteers in the community assisting with shared food plots, clearing streams of rubbish and even helping out at old folks' homes or daycare centres.

We established support groups for new immigrants so they felt welcome and assimilated more easily into a new culture.

As time passed, even the most indolent person saw the light and became involved. Families and communities became stronger as a result. People were healthier because they grew their own food and paradoxically crime drastically reduced because people felt more connected to their communities.

We tackled the health sector. We'd watched our parents lose their jobs and their self-worth. We'd watched them fall into depression; develop poor sleep patterns and crashed immune systems. Health specialists began working closely with the wellbeing centres to offer joint support as people dealt with the initial shock of job loss. They sought out and advertised volunteer opportunities where people could learn new skills and get their health and self-worth back on track.

However, the biggest shift we forced on the health sector was reinstating safe accommodation for people with mental health challenges. The days of pushing them out onto the streets was no longer acceptable.

We pestered governments to get in behind the all the initiatives so that departments worked together, not as isolated and costly silos, and the money saved was delivered back to the communities via the universal wage.

The massive imbalance of rich and poor was no longer tolerated.

We lobbied, bullied and cajoled until realistic taxes were paid by corporates and rich people alike. We dobbed in businesses that failed to pay appropriate wages. We named and shamed the businesses that failed to pay reasonable taxes. Taxes support local infrastructure.

Via social media we glowingly acknowledged organisations that invested in social responsibility.

Strangely, after about 20 years, we'd probably moved to what could best be described as The Age of Personal Responsibility. Changes in the education process had created a shift in thinking. Students no longer talked about getting a 'job', rather they took ownership of upskilling themselves. They no longer expected a job for life and no longer expected to be paid for sitting at home vegetating.

Here I am 50 years later, a grandmother myself. I suspect we've mutated into an Age of Personal Freedom.

Today's teachers now teach my grandchildren to 'do what you love; learn what excites you; follow your passion; follow your dream'. Special emphasis is put on helping others; contributing to society and giving back. Kids are blossoming. Some become entrepreneurs and create working opportunities (no longer called jobs). Others are happy to work flexi-time so they can spend time doing other things, like painting or writing.

The drive for more and more material things ebbed as society faced the enormous cost of human waste.

Crazy bonus packages for CEOs were removed about 10 years ago. Shareholders no longer tolerate CEOs who expect massive packages and then run their company into the ground.

We'd similarly made the green movement everyone's top priority. We wanted to ensure the next generations actually had a planet to inherit rather than some burnt-out husk where everything that made it beautiful had been destroyed in the quest for more and more useless 'stuff'.

I believe we took society to a whole new level of awareness and accountability.

I sit back on my porch and remember those dark days 50 years ago and I'm so proud of the outcome. I'm proud of my millennial mates; the kids who everyone said were lazy and pampered. I'm proud of the mums and grandmothers who supported us; the immigrants who taught us more than we ever taught them, and the gays and transgenders who similarly said 'We are of value.' Boy, did we make a difference.

The age of greed is declared officially over.

'The question isn't who is going to let me, the question is who is going to stop me?'

Ayn Rand

What is the world's what next?

As I was putting the finishing touches to this book, as often happens, I stumble across something so relevant to my message that it literally takes my breath away. I've long been a collector of American Indian wisdom and this story hit my inbox one day:

'The Rainbow Prophecy

'One day … there would come a time, when the earth being ravaged and polluted, the forests being destroyed, the birds would fall from the air, the waters would be blackened, the fish being poisoned in the streams, and the trees would no longer be, mankind as we would know it would all but cease to exist.

'There will come a day when people of all races, colours, and creeds will put aside their differences. They will come together in love, joining hands in unification, to heal the Earth and all Her children. They will move over the Earth like a great Whirling Rainbow, bringing peace, understanding and healing everywhere they go. Many creatures thought to be extinct or mythical will resurface at this time; the great trees that perished will return almost overnight. All living things will flourish, drawing sustenance from the breast of our Mother, the Earth.

'The great spiritual Teachers who walked the Earth and taught the basics of the truths of the Whirling Rainbow Prophecy will return and walk among us once more, sharing their power and understanding with all. We will learn how to see and hear in a sacred manner. Men and women will be equals in the way Creator intended them to be; all children will be safe anywhere they want to go. Elders will be respected and valued for their contributions to life. Their wisdom will be sought out. The whole Human race will be called The People and there will be no more war, sickness or hunger forever.'

'The Rainbow Prophecy' was retold by a woman from the Cree nation over a century ago. It refers to the keepers of the rituals and the values we urgently need to return to if we are to restore the damage we humans have caused and are continuing to cause. The prophecy goes on to say that people themselves will unite to create a world of justice, peace and freedom and be known as the 'Warriors of the Rainbow'.

Whether you believe in myths or legends, one thing is absolutely clear: we have only one planet and we are destroying it with our greed. No one leader can fix this; it is up to every one of us to work out our part in the destruction but also our part in the rebuilding of our planet for future generations.

One interesting aspect of the prophecy talks about the choosing of our leaders, and according to the prophecy, 'a leader will not be the one who talks the loudest, who boasts of success or has the support of the elite; leaders will be the ones whose action speak the loudest, people who have demonstrated wisdom and courage and have shown they work for the benefit of all'.

Grandfather William Commanda also prophesied a time he called 'The Seventh Fire', when new people would emerge. He predicted that a light-skinned race would be given the choice between two roads. One road is the road of greed without wisdom or respect for life, a road that will take us towards destruction; or we can choose another road, a road of spirituality, a slower road that includes respect for all living things.

I think we are at that point right now.

These prophecies are reflected in many cultures and we can look at them as quaint little fairy stories or we can listen to the underlying message. Corruption, elitism, consumerism, the rich getting richer while ordinary families struggle to survive, is not a recipe for a successful future for humankind and absolutely not a recipe for the sustainability of our planet.

There really is no Planet B.

At some stage all the pollution we are causing and our never-ending quest for more and more while we destroy the very things that sustain life, are utterly dumb. No matter how rich people become, they can't eat money, and all the wealth in the world is of no value if you have no water to drink; the seas have become so toxic all the fish are dead and we have destroyed all the forests that keep our air breathable.

> *'Here is your country. Cherish these natural wonders, cherish the natural resources, cherish the history and romance as a sacred heritage, for your children and your children's children. Do not let selfish men or greedy interests skin your country of its beauty, its riches or its romance.'*
>
> *Theodore Roosevelt*

What is *your* what next?

Helen Keller once said: 'I am only one, but still I am one. I cannot do everything, but still I can do something; and because I cannot do everything, I will not refuse to do something that I can do.'

As I was writing this book I kept an eye open for simple ways people could make a difference. Not everyone wants to be a warrior, but I believe in my heart that everyone wants to make a difference.

Caroline Salisbury watched the devastation in Vanuatu after Cyclone Pam in 2015 from the safety of her home in New Zealand. Caroline was then 65 years old. She didn't know anyone in Vanuatu; she wasn't a wealthy woman who could have sent a big donation; she was just one person who wanted to do something to help.

She went onto Facebook and asked people who made quilts to donate a quilt. Caroline ended up with over 700 beautiful quilts, which caused another problem: how to get that number of thick, large quilts up to Vanuatu. A month after the cyclone, the cruise ship *Pacific Pearl* agreed to take the quilts as part of the cyclone recovery effort, so Caroline went on the ship too. She wanted to personally hand over the quilts to the women of the villages.

In Port Vila one woman invited Caroline to meet her family, in particular she wanted to introduce her grandmother. Their home was literally a mud hut. A river had washed through the village, leaving mud in all the houses. Caroline went into the grandmother's hut to meet the old lady and noticed a very old, very rusty sewing machine sitting in the corner. Without any English, the grandmother indicated that when the village was flooded, her sewing machine ended up under water and was now useless.

As if donating the quilts wasn't enough, Caroline went back to New Zealand, hopped back onto Facebook and asked if anyone could donate sewing machines. She ended up with 21 machines, which necessitated another trip to the island. She contacted the Kiwanis, an organisation that regularly sent containers of desks and books to the islands, to see if they had space for the sewing machine along with as much fabric as she could beg and borrow. They were very willing to share the container space.

The initiative is now called 'Kiwanis: Threads across the Pacific'. A year later Caroline spoke to Bernina to see if they could help her purchase good basic sewing machines at a favourable cost; they were more than happy to help. The island now has 140 machines based in a local school where the women gather as groups to sew and chat.

That was five years ago; now Caroline and around eight helpers head up to the islands twice a year. They take up the next batch of sewing machines, fabric, thread and anything else they can load into containers to help the women create garments. Initially the women sewed for their families but as their skills improved, the women were able to create saleable garments. On a roster system, two of the women head to the coast with their products to sell to the many cruise ships that visit the island. Some women sell in the villages, some to the regular cruise ships, and one woman has created a small sewing school to carry on the teaching throughout the year.

The women of Vanuatu invariably have no form of income. The country is extremely poor and if their husbands die, desert the family, lose their jobs or can't find work, then there is no welfare system to help. The women are left to fend for themselves. Now these women are not only able to add to the family income but mothers can now afford to send their daughters to school. Affording an education is something most of the women in the villages have never been able to do.

Out of a cyclone, one woman changed the lives of women in several villages; she even changed the face of the villages, as now those women can earn an income. Their skills and endeavours will also pass on to the next generation.

I asked Caroline how she sourced her fabric. She told me that most days when she opens her front door, she will find a bundle of something she can use and so she starts filling her next container. A simple story of people helping people. Caroline says she is mindful of the old saying 'Give a man a fish and you feed his family for today, teach a man to fish and you feed them for a lifetime.'

Make Give Live NZ (remember the 'Archie Effect') 'is a social enterprise that connects and nurtures the wellbeing of people in their communities while crafting beautiful knitwear for you and people in need. Groups of people get together every week or two in their local cafe or community space to enjoy each other's company, a laugh and a cuppa and make a beautiful collection of beanies that we sell as 'buy one — give one' meaning for each one sold we give one to a Kiwi in need through a few charities. Our purpose is easing isolation and improving mental health and wellbeing through connection and the well-proven therapy of knitting and crochet.' So like Caroline's group, women meeting, creating, chatting and supporting each other, changing their own lives and making a difference.

A couple of people who attended a music festival noticed that literally hundreds of tents, tarpaulins and sleeping bags were abandoned once the festival was over. They gathered them all up, washed and cleaned them and are now sending them to people living in a refugee camp in Greece.

Start a community garden. A chance meeting with a neighbour kicked off a community vegetable garden project in north London. The local council became involved by handing out wildflower seeds. The seeds led to sharing plants, to someone writing a newsletter letting people know how to get involved. Fifty neighbours signed up to grow vegetables in their front gardens. The gardening project has brought a community together, where a multicultural community now regularly have joint gatherings to celebrate all manner of things.

Swap shops in the UK. This is another UK initiative. There are now swap shops in Bristol, Edinburgh, London, Manchester, Portsmouth and Southampton. Their website shows you how to set up a swap shop in your area.

Reverse Garbage Australia is a creative reuse centre making a difference in the world by reducing waste and creating change in the way we look at resources. They inspire and support kids, adults, artists and teachers to consume less, make more, save money — and feel good doing it!

This group is Australia based, but there is nothing to stop anyone doing the same thing in their area. This group ensures the materials people donate end up with people who can turn them into something useful or artistic. Their aim is to 'reduce waste costs so your stuff doesn't end up in landfills. It reduces your carbon footprint by donating your leftovers which in turn avoids the energy and waste generation associated with recycling'.

San Antonia, USA. School kids in the local high school take dogs from the local animal shelter on their early-morning cross-country runs. According to their coach, he couldn't work out who had more fun, the kids or the dogs.

> *'Don't wait until everything is just right. It will never be perfect. There will always be challenges, obstacles, and less than perfect conditions. So what? Get started now. With each step you take, you will grow stronger and stronger, more and more skilled, more and more self-confident, and more and more successful.'*
>
> *Mark Victor Hansen*

Will you feel the fear and do it anyway?

Feel the Fear and Do It Anyway has to be the best book title ever. Whenever I have doubts about doing something, I think of that title and it kick-starts me.

It's human nature for us to hope that someone else will fix things; sometimes they do, often they don't.

Imagine if you could make a difference. Imagine if you could get a small group of equally concerned, excited, energised people together to tackle an issue. Imagine what you could do if you became a kitchen table warrior. What would you choose? Where would you start?

Some people feel too shy to start a group and may prefer to tackle things alone. As women we usually do the bulk of the shopping, so we make our protest as we ensure we purchase goods from ethical companies and ethical countries. At best we can avoid supporting the Nestlés and the Cadburys and the Hershey's of this world.

If you think about the 'Archie' groups, those women joined together to knit and crochet as much for their own mental health and/or isolation and loneliness as they did for knitting hats, and that's okay. There's a whole lot of loneliness in the world.

At the back of this book I've listed numerous organisations you can join but if you would prefer to start your own small group, that's okay also.

Go well. Be brave. Get going.

> *'The dream begins with a teacher, someone who pushes you and pokes you with a big stick called "truth".'*
>
> *Goethe*

Final discussion questions

Which chapter was of the most interest to you?

Why was that?

Which 'warrior' woman did you most relate to?

Why?

What was your 'destiny' number?

Does that excite you or terrify you?

Are you fulfilling your destiny?

What aspect of your community concerns you?

What could you do to raise awareness of that issue?

I ask again, is there already a group you could join?

I ask again, would you be willing to start your own group?

Who could you invite to join you?

When will you start?

Bonus quotes

'Sometimes you have to make a decision that will break your heart but give peace to your soul.' Unknown

'Karma comes after everyone eventually. You can't get away with screwing people over your whole life. I don't care who you are. What goes around comes around. That's how it works. Sooner or later the universe will serve you the revenge that you deserve.' Jessica Brody

'Vengeance is the act of turning anger in on yourself. On the surface it may be directed at someone else, but it's a sure–fire recipe for arresting emotional recovery.' Jane Goldman

'As women, we must speak out, speak up, say no to our inheritance of loss and yes to a future of women-led dialogue about women's rights and value.' Zainab Salbi

'I've been absolutely terrified every moment of my life — and I've never let it keep me from doing a single thing I wanted to do.' Georgia O'Keeffe

'The most courageous act is still to think for yourself. Aloud.' Coco Chanel

'I can honestly say that I was never affected by the question of the success of an undertaking. If I felt it was the right thing to do, I was for it regardless of the possible outcome.' Golda Meir

"Tell me not to do something and I'll do it twice and take pictures!' Not known

'Yes, he's an idiot with zero common sense, but he IS my son. I just hope he never goes into politics, he'd be a disaster.' Mary Anne Trump

'Why aren't crazy people content to take over, like, one town? It always has to be the whole world. They can't just control maybe twenty people,

they have to control everyone. They can't just be stinking rich. They can't just do genetic experiments on a couple unlucky few. They have to put something in the water. In the air. To get everyone. I was tired of all of it.' James Patterson, *Angel*

'When they discover the centre of the universe, a lot of people will be disappointed to discover they are not it.' Bernard Bailey

'Beginning today, treat everyone you meet as if they were going to be dead by midnight. Extend to them all the care, kindness and understanding you can muster, and do it with no thought of any reward. Your life will never be the same again.' Og Mandino

'Be yourself; everyone else is taken.' Oscar Wilde

'MEN — if you want to know what a woman's mind feels like, imagine a browser with 2857 tabs open all the time.' Not known

'A word of encouragement during failure is worth more than an hour of praise after success.' Unknown

'Power is always dangerous. Power attracts the worst and corrupts the best.' Edward Abbey

'If women took up arms to defend their reproductive rights, the GOP would ban assault rifles yesterday.' Steve Marmel

'Corruption is a cancer that steals from the poor, eats away at governance and moral fiber and destroys trust.' Robert Zoellick

'As long as greed is stronger than compassion, there will always be suffering.' Rusty Eric

'Democracy is the worst form of government except for all the others.' Winston Churchill

'I'm tired of hearing that democracy doesn't work. Of course it doesn't work, we are supposed to work it.' Alexander Woollcott

'In a democracy you believe it or not, in a dictatorship you believe it or else.' Evan Esar

'Democracy is not the law of the majority, but the protection of the minority.' Albert Camus

'Man's capacity for justice makes democracy possible, man's inclination to injustice makes democracy necessary.' Reinhold Niebuhr

'Being a woman is a terribly difficult task since it consists primarily in dealing with men.' Joseph Conrad

RESOURCES

How to set up a swap shop:

https://www.theguardian.com/lifeandstyle/2014/sep/15/how-to-set-up-clothes-swap-in-your-area

How to set up a community garden:

http://www.ccga.org.nz/uploads/Guide_to_starting_a_Community_Garden.pdf

How to set up a community group:

http://www.takepart.org/contentControl/documentControl/12494_12470_how%20to%20set%20up%20a%20community%20group.pdf

Caroline invites you to learn more and to see how you can contribute to the women of Vanuatu by following the story on her Facebook page 'Kiwanis: Threads across the Pacific'.

FURTHER READING

Lessons in Leadership: 50 ways to avoid falling into the 'Trump' trap by Ann Andrews

Leaders Behaving Badly: What happens when ordinary people show up, stand up and speak up by Ann Andrews

The Third Wave by Alvin Toffler

Feel the Fear and Do It Anyway by Susan Jeffers

The Life You Were Born To Live by Dan Millman

NB: *The Future Seekers* by Kimberley Patterson appears to be no longer in print, however Dan Millman's book *The Life You Were Born To Live* is an even more in-depth way of working out your destiny number and your life path.

REFERENCES

Introduction

https://en.wikipedia.org/wiki/Gladys_Aylward

https://en.wikipedia.org/wiki/
The_Inn_of_the_Sixth_Happiness

The story of foot binding: https://www.theatlantic.com/china/archive/2013/09/the-peculiar-history-of-foot-binding-in-china/279718/

https://en.wikipedia.org/wiki/
Japanese_invasion_of_Manchuria

https://www.businessinsider.com.au/watch-christine-blasey-ford-accepts-aclu-award-for-courage-2019-11

https://www.biography.com/scientist/florence-nightingale

https://www.natgeokids.com/nz/discover/history/general-history/edith-cavell/

Chapter 1: How women have already shaped the world

https://en.wikipedia.org/wiki/Orson_Scott_Card

https://en.wikipedia.org/wiki/Great_Depression

https://www.tupperware.com/

https://en.wikipedia.org/wiki/Women%27s_suffrage_in_the_United_Kingdom

https://en.wikipedia.org/wiki/Suffragette

https://en.wikipedia.org/wiki/Emily_Davison

https://www.huffpost.com/entry/female-hysteria_n_4298060

https://en.wikipedia.org/wiki/Emmeline_Pankhurst

https://en.wikipedia.org/wiki/Eleanor_Roosevelt

https://en.wikipedia.org/wiki/Rosie_the_Riveter

https://hbr.org/cover-story/2019/09/gender-equality-is-within-our-reach

https://www.quora.com/In-which-countries-do-women-not-have-a-right-to-vote

Smaller brains: https://www.bbc.com/news/blogs-trending-41361123

Chapter 2: There's work to be done and woman will do it

https://www.goodreads.com/author/show/1391130.Shannon_L_Alder

https://en.wikipedia.org/wiki/Jane_Goodall

https://en.wikipedia.org/wiki/Ruth_Bader_Ginsburg

https://www.cnbc.com/2019/12/19/ruth-bader-ginsberg-says-young-people-keep-her-optimistic-about-future.html

https://en.wikipedia.org/wiki/Christine_Blasey_Ford

https://en.wikipedia.org/wiki/Brett_Kavanaugh

https://en.wikipedia.org/wiki/Michelle_Obama

https://en.wikipedia.org/wiki/Jacinda_Ardern

https://en.wikipedia.org/wiki/Christchurch_mosque_shootings

https://www.npr.org/2019/04/10/711820023/new-zealand-passes-law-banning-most-semi-automatic-weapons

https://www.newshub.co.nz/home/politics/2019/03/global-alliance-jacinda-ardern-joins-world-leaders-calling-for-tech-giant-accountability.html

https://www.theguardian.com/world/2019/may/13/christchurch-call-details-emerge-of-arderns-plan-to-tackle-online-extremism

https://www.theguardian.com/world/2019/may/15/jacinda-ardern-emmanuel-macron-christchurch-call-summit-extremist-violence-online

https://www.stuff.co.nz/national/politics/112160697/jacinda-ardern-second-in-fortune-magazines-worlds-greatest-leaders-list

https://en.wikipedia.org/wiki/Anita_Roddick

https://www.independent.co.uk/news/uk/this-britain/anita-roddick-capitalist-with-a-conscience-dies-at-64-402014.htmlhttps://www.theguardian.com/news/2007/sep/12/guardianobituaries.business

https://en.wikipedia.org/wiki/Melinda_Gates

https://www.cnbc.com/2018/05/21/2018s-fortune-500-companies-have-just-24-female-ceos.html

https://www.vox.com/policy-and-politics/2018/11/7/18024742/midterm-results-record-women-win

https://en.wikipedia.org/wiki/Melinda_Gates

https://en.wikipedia.org/wiki/Linda_Ronstadt

https://en.wikipedia.org/wiki/Lloyd_Groff_Copeman

https://en.wikipedia.org/wiki/Elissa_Slotkin

https://www.theguardian.com/us-news/2018/nov/16/the-democratic-blue-wave-was-real

https://en.wikipedia.org/wiki/Elizabeth_Warren

https://elizabethwarren.com/plans

https://en.wikipedia.org/wiki/Malala_Yousafzai

https://en.wikipedia.org/wiki/Fatwa

https://en.unesco.org/news/unesco-and-pakistan-launch-malala-fund-girls-education

https://en.wikipedia.org/wiki/Angela_Merkel

https://www.britannica.com/biography/Angela-Merkel

https://www.bundeskanzlerin.de/bkin-en/medal-of-freedom-as-a-tribute-to-angela-merkel-s-life-achievement-607586

https://en.wikipedia.org/wiki/J._K._Rowling

https://mashable.com/2018/05/10/j-k-rowling-donald-trump-signature/

https://www.handwriting-graphology.com/study-of-handwriting/

https://mashable.com/2017/01/20/j-k-rowling-best-donald-trump-twitter-burns/

https://www.huffpost.com/entry/jk-rowling-trolls-donald-trump-with-perfect-response-to-his-latest-tweet_n_5b3bf42de4b05127cced6695

https://en.wikipedia.org/wiki/Bette_Midler

https://en.wikipedia.org/wiki/The_Rose_(film)

https://en.wikipedia.org/wiki/Donald_Trump_Access_Hollywood_tape

https://www.theguardian.com/stage/2019/jun/05/bette-midler-trump-twitter-feud-latest

https://en.wikipedia.org/wiki/Emma_Gonz%C3%A1lez

https://edition.cnn.com/2018/02/17/us/florida-student-emma-gonzalez-speech/index.html

https://variety.com/2018/biz/news/emma-gonzalez-gun-violence-victims-power-of-women-1202978914/

https://en.wikipedia.org/wiki/Alexandria_Ocasio-Cortez

https://en.wikipedia.org/wiki/Green_New_Deal

https://www.businessinsider.com.au/alexandria-ocasio-cortez-aoc-facebook-mark-zuckerberg-meme-italian-godfather-2019-10?r=US&IR=T

https://www.businessinsider.com.au/aoc-mark-zuckerberg-video-congress-facebook-questioning-2019-10

https://www.theguardian.com/us-news/2019/dec/24/alexandria-ocasio-cortez-aoc-first-year-congress

https://en.wikipedia.org/wiki/Jane_Fonda

https://en.wikipedia.org/wiki/Women%27s_Media_Center

https://www.etonline.com/jane-fondas-climate-change-protests-a-timeline-of-her-fire-drill-fridays-and-multiple-arrests

https://en.wikipedia.org/wiki/Lucy_Lawless

http://www.stuff.co.nz/business/industries/6482880/Lucy-Lawless-released-after-Shell-oil-protest-arrest

https://www.nzherald.co.nz/nz/news/article.cfm?c_id=1&objectid=10863945

https://www.greenpeace.org/international/press-release/7449/actress-lucy-lawless-joins-climate-change-survivor-in-protest-against-arctic-exploitation-for-norwegian-oil/

https://www.greenpeace.org/international/story/24426/a-letter-to-shell-for-taking-away-my-family-and-devastating-my-community/

https://www.stuff.co.nz/entertainment/celebrities/114444513/xena-star-lucy-lawless-is-brutally-disappointed-in-her-generation?rm=m

https://en.wikipedia.org/wiki/Louise_Hay

Chronic fatigue: https://www.cdc.gov/me-cfs/symptoms-diagnosis/index.html

https://en.wikipedia.org/wiki/Oprah_Winfrey

https://www.britannica.com/biography/Oprah-Winfrey

https://en.wikipedia.org/wiki/The_Color_Purple_(film)

https://en.wikipedia.org/wiki/Harpo_Productions

https://en.wikipedia.org/wiki/Before_Women_Had_Wings

https://en.wikipedia.org/wiki/Beloved_(novel)

https://en.wikipedia.org/wiki/Selma_(film)

https://www.oprah.com/pressroom/about-oprahs-angel-network

https://obamawhitehouse.archives.gov/blog/2013/11/20/president-obama-honors-presidential-medal-freedom-recipients

https://en.wikipedia.org/wiki/Marie_Yovanovitch

https://en.wikipedia.org/wiki/Rudy_Giuliani

https://en.wikipedia.org/wiki/Gordon_Sondland

https://en.wikipedia.org/wiki/Joe_Biden

https://www.reuters.com/article/us-hunter-biden-ukraine/what-hunter-biden-did-on-the-board-of-ukrainian-energy-company-burisma-idUSKBN1WX1P7

https://en.wikipedia.org/wiki/Burisma_Holdings

https://en.wikipedia.org/wiki/Trump%E2%80%93Ukraine_scandal

https://www.cnbc.com/2019/10/12/i-would-like-you-to-do-us-a-favor-the-30-minute-phone-call-that-changed-trumps-presidency.html

https://www.businessinsider.com.au/trump-zelensky-ukraine-call-transcript-quid-pro-quo-biden-2019-9?r=US&IR=T

https://www.kusi.com/i/the-latest-yovanovitch-told-to-return-on-the-next-plane/

https://www.npr.org/2019/11/15/776987555/impeachment-hearings-continue-with-marie-yovanovitch-ex-ambassador-to-ukraine

https://www.pbs.org/newshour/politics/white-house-defends-trump-tweets-about-yovanovitch-during-hearing

https://www.reuters.com/article/us-usa-trump-impeachment-quotes-factbox/youre-tough-as-nails-and-youre-smart-as-hell-quotes-from-trump-impeachment-hearing-idUSKBN1XP1KY

https://en.wikipedia.org/wiki/Fiona_Hill_(presidential_advisor)

https://www.thenation.com/article/archive/fiona-hill-impeachment-testimony/

https://thebulwark.com/fiona-hill-impeachment-queen/

https://en.wikipedia.org/wiki/Kamala_Harris

https://www.nytimes.com/video/us/politics/100000005162877/senator-kamala-harris-questions-jeff-sessions.html

https://nymag.com/intelligencer/2019/05/cory-booker-tries-not-to-laugh-as-kamala-harris-grills-barr.html

https://www.thecut.com/2018/09/kamala-harriss-abortion-questions-left-kavanaugh-speechless.html#_ga=2.169818913.1414026534.1583444354-1380511288.1583444354

https://www.usatoday.com/story/news/politics/onpolitics/2017/06/13/social-media-lights-up-after-kamala-harris-questions-jeff-sessions/102824106/

https://www.thedailybeast.com/sessions-to-kamala-harris-youre-making-me-nervous

https://www.msnbc.com/msnbc/watch/watch-sen-harris-showing-off-prosecutorial-prowess-puts-ag-barr-on-his-heels-1515668547555

https://en.wikipedia.org/wiki/Nancy_Pelosi

https://www.theguardian.com/us-news/2019/feb/06/nancy-pelosi-clap-trump-photo-state-of-the-union

https://www.inquirer.com/politics/nation/nancy-pelosi-dont-mess-with-me-press-conference-20191205.html

https://edition.cnn.com/2020/02/04/politics/rush-limbaugh-donald-trump-medal-of-freedom/index.html

https://www.nbcnews.com/think/opinion/nancy-pelosi-tears-trump-s-state-union-speech-possible-2020-ncna1130776

https://www.reuters.com/article/us-usa-trump-speech-pelosi/u-s-speaker-pelosi-says-she-ripped-up-trump-speech-because-it-shredded-the-truth-idUSKBN1ZZ2O3

https://en.wikipedia.org/wiki/Greta_Thunberg

Greta's dad: https://www.bbc.com/news/uk-50901789

https://www.heraldsun.com.au/blogs/andrew-bolt/the-disturbing-secret-to-the-cult-of-greta-thunberg/news-story/55822063e3589e02707fbb5a9a75d4cc

https://www.theguardian.com/australia-news/2019/sep/25/morrison-responds-to-greta-thunberg-speech-by-warning-children-against-needless-climate-anxiety

https://www.irishtimes.com/life-and-style/people/why-is-greta-thunberg-so-triggering-for-certain-men-1.4002264

https://time.com/person-of-the-year-2019-greta-thunberg/

Chapter 3: How men set the table

https://en.wikipedia.org/wiki/Paternalism

https://www.bl.uk/romantics-and-victorians/articles/child-labour

https://www.worldatlas.com/articles/worst-countries-for-child-labor.htmlhttps://www.careeraddict.com/10-companies-that-still-use-child-labor

https://en.wikipedia.org/wiki/Margaret_Sanger

https://en.wikipedia.org/wiki/John_Stuart_Mill

https://en.wikipedia.org/wiki/Evangelicalism

https://www.vox.com/2018/5/18/17367964/trump-abortion-planned-parenthood-defund

https://en.wikipedia.org/wiki/Planned_Parenthood

https://www.npr.org/2019/05/22/725634053/anti-abortion-rights-groups-push-gop-to-rethink-rape-and-incest-exceptions

https://www.npr.org/2019/05/14/723312937/alabama-lawmakers-passes-abortion-ban

https://www.theatlantic.com/health/archive/2018/10/how-many-women-die-illegal-abortions/572638/

https://en.wikipedia.org/wiki/Roe_v._Wade

https://en.wikipedia.org/wiki/Richard_Nixon

https://www.who.int/news-room/fact-sheets/detail/preventing-unsafe-abortion

https://en.wikipedia.org/wiki/Abortion_in_the_Republic_of_Ireland

https://en.wikipedia.org/wiki/Conservatism

https://okieblog.wordpress.com/2012/06/05/what-is-conservatism-and-what-is-wrong-with-it/https://www.sbs.com.au/news/scott-morrison-says-the-rise-of-women-should-not-come-at-the-expense-of-men

https://en.wikipedia.org/wiki/Angry_white_male

https://qz.com/1719873/greta-thunberg-comes-under-attack-from-misogynistic-men/

https://www.notredame.edu.au/about/schools/sydney/arts-and-sciences/school-staff/camilla-nelson

https://www.theguardian.com/australia-news/2019/sep/25/morrison-responds-to-greta-thunberg-speech-by-warning-children-against-needless-climate-anxiety

https://en.wikipedia.org/wiki/William_Golding

https://en.wikipedia.org/wiki/Daniel_Craig

https://en.wikipedia.org/wiki/Benedict_Cumberbatch

https://en.wikipedia.org/wiki/John_Legend

https://en.wikipedia.org/wiki/Ashton_Kutcher

Chapter 4: Why doing what we've always done no longer works

https://en.wikipedia.org/wiki/Feminism

https://www.goodhousekeeping.com/life/g28470640/best-feminist-quotes/

https://en.wikipedia.org/wiki/Gloria_Steinem

https://en.wikipedia.org/wiki/Feminism#19th_and_early-20th_centuries

https://msmagazine.com/

https://www.huffingtonpost.ca/2017/09/27/women-chores-home_a_23224733/

https://en.wikipedia.org/wiki/Ford_sewing_machinists_strike_of_1968

https://inews.co.uk/news/long-reads/women-showing-anger-is-ok-about-time-too-224132

The Encyclopedia of Psychology

https://www.nytimes.com/2018/01/17/magazine/i-used-to-insist-i-didnt-get-angry-not-anymore.html

https://electricliterature.com/why-arent-women-allowed-to-be-angry/

https://en.wikipedia.org/wiki/Leslie_Jamison

https://en.wikipedia.org/wiki/Hillary_Clinton

https://en.wikipedia.org/wiki/What_Happened_(Clinton_book)

https://time.com/5777514/women-wearing-white-state-of-the-union/

https://www.huffpost.com/entry/celebrity-feminism-2010-taylor-swift_n_5dfbdc44e4b006dceaab16a7

https://en.wikipedia.org/wiki/Taylor_Swift

https://www.ted.com/talks/chimamanda_ngozi_adichie_the_danger_of_a_single_story

https://en.wikipedia.org/wiki/Megyn_Kelly

https://en.wikipedia.org/wiki/Chimamanda_Ngozi_Adichie

Chapter 5: Greed is *not* good

https://en.wikipedia.org/wiki/Capitalism

https://www.forbes.com/sites/stevedenning/2017/07/17/making-sense-of-shareholder-value-the-worlds-dumbest-idea/#18f729b42a7e

https://en.wikipedia.org/wiki/Jack_Welch

https://hbr.org/2017/05/managing-for-the-long-term

https://www.economist.com/business/2016/03/31/analyse-this

https://en.wikipedia.org/wiki/Milton_Friedman

https://en.wikipedia.org/wiki/Trickle-down_economics

https://www.cnbc.com/2019/08/19/the-ceos-of-nearly-two-hundred-companies-say-shareholder-value-is-no-longer-their-main-objective.html

https://eom.org/bruno-roche

https://eom.org/content-hub-blog/ceos-turning-away-from-only-prioritising-shareholder-value

https://www.ethicalconsumer.org/

https://www.inc.com/business-insider/ceos-new-york-times-ad-apple-amazon-walmart-social-responsibility-profits.html

https://longreads.com/2017/10/04/nestle-is-sucking-the-worlds-aquifers-dry/ https://www.snopes.com/fact-check/nestle-ceo-water-not-human-right/
https://www.globalresearch.ca/the-complete-history-of-monsanto-the-worlds-most-evil-corporation/5387964

https://www.theguardian.com/technology/2019/apr/02/revealed-amazon-employees-suffer-after-workplace-injuries

https://www.motherjones.com/environment/2017/12/amazon-pretends-to-care-about-climate-until-its-time-to-build-a-new-headquarters/ https://www.theguardian.com/business/2014/oct/29/serious-fraud-office-investigate-tesco

https://www.commondreams.org/newswire/2008/09/12/coca-cola-continues-unethical-and-dishonest-practices-india

https://www.marketwatch.com/story/how-trumps-tax-cuts-helped-the-waltons-vs-walmart-workers-2018-11-06

https://www.huffpost.com/entry/walmart-environmentalism_n_5907524ae4b02655f83eba40

https://www.independent.co.uk/environment/orangutans-palm-oil-habitat-rainforest-cadbury-mondelez-oreos-indonesia-greenpeace-a8630801.html

https://www.mirror.co.uk/news/uk-news/red-cross-sexual-misconduct-scandal-12082766

https://www.propublica.org/article/how-the-red-cross-raised-half-a-billion-dollars-for-haiti-and-built-6-homes

https://www.npr.org/2015/06/03/411524156/in-search-of-the-red-cross-500-million-in-haiti-relief

https://plan-international.org/

https://en.wikipedia.org/wiki/Oxfam

Chapter 6: You can move a mountain one rock at a time or by causing a giant avalanche

https://en.wikipedia.org/wiki/Liberalism

https://en.wikipedia.org/wiki/Socialism

https://www.google.com/search?q=definition+of+capitalism&oq=definition+of+capitalism&aqs=chrome..69i57j0l7.8310j1j4&sourceid=chrome&ie=UTF-8

https://en.wikipedia.org/wiki/Communism

https://en.wikipedia.org/wiki/Social_democracy

https://www.eiu.com/topic/democracy-index

https://www.usatoday.com/story/money/nation-now/2016/02/09/french-supermarkets-must-now-donate-unsold-food-charity/80076632/

https://www.globalcitizen.org/en/content/ethiopia-tree-planting-record/

https://www.communityfoundations.ca/our-purpose/
https://www.signupgenius.com/nonprofit/community-service-project-ideas.cfm

https://www.theanimalclub.net/dogs/high-school-cross-country-team-brings-local-shelter-dogs-along-on-their-morning-run/

https://www.globalcitizen.org/en/content/chile-10-million-acres-national-parks-patagonia/

https://www.goodshomedesign.com/kenya-installs-the-first-solar-plant-that-transforms-ocean-water-into-drinking-water/

https://www.disclose.tv/farmers-return-to-ancient-method-fighting-pests-by-planting-wildflowers-instead-of-using-chemicals-381991

Chapter 7: Have you fulfilled your destiny? If not, why not?

https://en.wikipedia.org/wiki/Suzanne_Collins

https://en.wikipedia.org/wiki/Tarana_Burke

https://en.wikipedia.org/wiki/Harvey_Weinstein

https://en.wikipedia.org/wiki/Me_Too_movement

https://en.wikipedia.org/wiki/Alyssa_Milano

https://en.wikipedia.org/wiki/Time%27s_Up_(movement)

https://time.com/time-person-of-the-year-2017-silence-breakers/

https://en.wikipedia.org/wiki/Roy_Moore

https://en.wikipedia.org/wiki/Doug_Jones_(politician)

https://time.com/5018813/farmworkers-solidarity-hollywood-sexual-assault/

https://en.wikipedia.org/wiki/Mark_Wahlberg

Fight to the death: https://www.bbc.com/news/world-latin-america-51489961

https://en.wikipedia.org/wiki/Melanne_Verveer

https://www.un.org/en/events/pastevents/women_conf_beijing_1995.shtml

https://www.nationalgeographic.com/culture/2019/10/peril-progress-prosperity-womens-well-being-around-the-world-feature/

https://iwda.org.au/take-action/international-womens-day/

https://data.unwomen.org/progress-of-the-worlds-women

https://en.wikipedia.org/wiki/Ellen_DeGeneres

https://chasekraynickpayitforward.wordpress.com/2012/10/03/pay-it-forward-where-did-this-idea-come-from-anyway/

https://en.wikipedia.org/wiki/Catherine_Ryan_Hyde

https://www.xero.com/blog/2015/04/getting-behind-the-pay-it-forward-movement/

https://globalpayitforwardday.com/

https://www.randomactsofkindness.org/

https://en.wikipedia.org/wiki/Anne_Herbert_(writer)

https://www.randomactsofkindness.org/kindness-ideas

https://en.wikipedia.org/wiki/Random_Acts_of_Kindness_Day

https://www.harpersbazaar.com/uk/fashion/fashion-news/a30386813/baby-archie-beanie/

https://makegivelive.co.nz/

https://en.wikipedia.org/wiki/2008%E2%80%932011_Icelandic_financial_crisis

https://muckrack.com/ruth-sunderland

https://grapevine.is/news/2018/02/07/36-bankers-96-years-in-jail/

https://www.theguardian.com/world/2009/feb/22/iceland-women

https://news.bitcoin.com/australian-banks-fraudulently-collected-fees-from-deceased-customers/

https://www.theguardian.com/australia-news/2019/nov/23/after-a-litany-of-bank-scandals-the-westpac-allegations-are-a-new-low

https://www.merriam-webster.com/dictionary/woke

Chapter 8: If not me, then who? If not now, then when?

https://www.taen.org.uk/

https://en.wikipedia.org/wiki/The_Third_Wave_(Toffler_book)

https://upliftconnect.com/rainbow-prophecy/

https://worldwidewisdomdirectory.com/blog/the-warriors-of-the-rainbow-prophecy.html http://www.anishinabenation.ca/en/history/william-commanda/

https://makegivelive.co.nz/

https://www.thetentcollectors.co.nz/

https://www.theguardian.com/lifeandstyle/2013/mar/15/gardens-community-vegetable-growing

https://reversegarbage.org.au/

https://www.theguardian.com/lifeandstyle/2014/sep/15/how-to-set-up-clothes-swap-in-your-area

https://www.runnersworld.com/news/a20817598/watch-high-school-cross-country-team-takes-shelter-dogs-on-training-run/

ABOUT THE AUTHOR

I spent four amazing years in the Women's Royal Navy, mostly working with the Royal Marines. I worked in a rather boring department — pay and records — which is where certain highly trained members of the marines would be stationed as they waited for the call-up to go wherever a conflict situation arose. They were the equivalent of what we now know as the SAS.

People still needed to be paid no matter how many staff we had left in these departments once the Marines had been shipped out. The armed forces pride themselves on the records they keep of every member of the forces, so in order for everything to function in their absence, we would all swap jobs every three to six months so we could step into any job at a moment's notice. It seemed to me to be such a simple and logical way to work and became the platform for the work I facilitated when working with teams in various organisations when I became a consultant.

After my contract with the Navy ended, I experienced a few civilian jobs, which showed me that not all businesses/organisations work the same way.

I briefly trained as a work study engineer with Johnson &

Johnson, a position which fascinated and horrified me; people being watched and timed as they did their job so we, the engineers, could work out how they could work faster and more efficiently.

In time I became a full-time mum to my son and daughter.

As they were growing up, I trained as a 'listener' with the Citizens Advice Bureau. Our job was just that — to listen to people who came to us with a problem, to help and advise them on their next step. Their problems could be anything as simple as wanting to know bus times to presenting with more serious issues. It was our job to listen to them; to hear them out and to then refer them to a specialist counsellor if that was deemed appropriate.

Often just having someone to listen to them was all that people under stress needed.

I loved helping people so decided to train as a counsellor myself. I subsequently trained in marriage guidance counselling and later in Neuro-linguistic Programming (NLP) techniques.

After 17 years, my own marriage broke down and I found myself a solo mum with one teenager and one soon-to-be-teenager; a dog that ate everyone's shoes, and a battered old car that used more oil than petrol. I also had to face the fact that I had obsolete skills and a desperate financial need to get back into the workforce so I could pay the mortgage and feed us.

We were hit hard with the breakdown of our family and the financial challenges were enormous. It was particularly hard for us all to take on board these changed financial circumstances; difficulties which were compounded when I had no choice but to find full-time work in order to support us. So on top of the financial woes, they now had a mum they hardly saw.

The end result was two sad and confused kids who started

displaying some pretty out-of-control behaviours as we all dealt with the pain and confusion of our new situation.

It was at this stage of my life that I heard about the concept of 'Toughlove', a movement which started in the USA to help families deal with solutions to unacceptable behaviours. Behaviours which, in some cases, were tearing their families apart.

The basic concept is that parents would get together weekly and talk through whatever issues they were struggling with, and by sharing their stories and hearing how other people had dealt with similar challenges, they were encouraged and supported to try different strategies. By having the backing and support of other parents, new people in the group would feel more confident to be able to deal with all manner of behaviours they felt totally unprepared for.

There were no groups in our area so to learn more about them I attended a public meeting and ended up joining forces with a school guidance counsellor to set up a group in our local area. It was a life-saver. I learned so much not only from the Toughlove philosophies, but also from other parents who had risked trying out scary new behaviours in order to stay sane during the painful teen years. These parents had succeeded in changing not only their kids' behaviours, but their own.

Meanwhile, on the job front, I took on a variety of low-skilled and low-paid jobs so I could pick up the skills required for a whole new computer age born in my years out of the workplace.

I subsequently became PA to a personnel manager; a man who saw things in me no-one else had ever seen and so despite my rusty skills, he trained me in all aspects of personnel management.

When he was eventually made redundant, I was offered the job as personnel officer — a seriously diminished version of his role and responsibilities, but a situation that presented me with a huge dilemma: my loyalty to a man who had trained me versus my desire to take on the role.

With his absolute encouragement I took the job.

I then had a fast-track career from personnel officer to personnel and industrial relations manager for a manufacturing company, to HR manager for a computer company and my ultimately terrifying decision to become an HR consultant in my own right.

As an HR consultant I've worked with businesses of all shapes and sizes, all colours and creeds. I specialised in working with high-performing teams sharing with them the strategies I'd learned while working with the Royal Marines and while learning the principles of work study.

I also worked in the areas of change management, performance management, succession planning and leadership. I've worked in areas as diverse as manufacturing and banking, technology and the health sector.

I trained as a 'profiler' to better help organisations recruit the right people for their culture. Understanding a person's personality via profiling also helped managers make more effective decisions with promotion and even with career direction and motivation. I talk about profiling in Chapter 7.

During the 30-plus years I worked in HR, I found it amazing that some of the techniques I had learned in counselling, marriage guidance and even Toughlove were totally transferable into the workplace. After all, there isn't much difference between a parent feeling powerless to deal with a teenager and a manager feeling powerless to know how to deal with a recalcitrant employee. And, similarly, there isn't a great deal of difference between an employee trying to get 'heard' by a manager and a teenager trying to put his or her point of view to a parent who grew up in a different era.

Parenting is a tough job; leadership is also a tough job. However, parenting and leadership come with certain responsibilities, and watching what is transpiring around the world has caused me such concern that I feel the absolute need to challenge what some people appear to think leadership is (unabridged power) and what it isn't (unabridged power).

'Pain travels through families until someone is ready to feel it.'

Stephi Wagner

ACKNOWLEDGEMENTS

Firstly, a huge thanks to Hannah, my lovely neighbour who set off this whole book. Thanks to Linda, Robyn and Ros who became my beta readers and gave me open and honest feedback. I absolutely valued that.

Thanks to my women's groups: Janice, Leigh, Thelma, Clare and Pam for their never-ending support and encouragement even when they think I've probably lost the plot.

Thanks to the amazing women in our local book club who opened up a whole new world of female authors to me after a lifetime of reading almost exclusively male, business books.

A massive thanks to Megan who introduced me to Caroline Salisbury. Caroline is an ordinary woman in her mid-60s who, from the safety of her home here in New Zealand, watched the devastation in Vanuatu from Cyclone Pam in 2015. This amazing woman knew no-one in Vanuatu. She isn't wealthy so couldn't just send a hefty cheque to assuage her concerns; yet against all logical odds, she has changed the lives of the women of Vanuatu and epitomises everything this book is about.

Thanks to the many women and men who gave me feedback on the cover. Special thanks to Martin, my very patient publisher; Eva, my even more patient editor. A massive thanks to Nick from Signature Press who translates my thoughts into the most beautiful covers; and finally, to Warren, my husband, who cooks for me and puts up with my mental absences when I'm knee deep in wrestling with a particularly tricky story.

OTHER BOOKS BY THE AUTHOR

Shift Your But (Self-published 1999)

Finding the Square Root of a Banana (Self-published 2000)

Did I Really Employ You? (Published by Reed Publishing (NZ), 2004)

Excellent Employment: Hiring the best people to help your business grow (Published by A & C Black, UK, 2007)

Mum's the Word by Vanessa Sunde, Kenina Court and Ann Andrews (Published by Phantom Publishing, 2007)

Lessons in Leadership: 50 Way to Avoid Falling into the 'Trump' Trap (Published by Moreau Publishing, 2017)

Leaders Behaving Badly: What happens when ordinary people show up, stand up and speak up (Published by Activity Press, 2018)

My Dear Franchisees, 2nd Edition (Activity Press 2019). First published 2006.

www.ingramcontent.com/pod-product-compliance
Lightning Source LLC
Chambersburg PA
CBHW060037030426
42334CB00019B/2369
9780473525026